W9-CSQ-254

Student Book

Blueprint

3

A2 Pre-Intermediate

Eric Williams · Peggy Anderson

Contents

Grammar and Structures	Listening / Reading	Writing / Speaking
Lesson 1 Present continuous for future plans	**L**: A radio interview	**W&S**: Talking about plans for next month and next semester
Lesson 2 Simple present vs. present continuous	**R**: A career flyer	**W&S**: Conversations between career counselors and job seekers/ students
Lesson 3 Gerunds and infinitives; conjunction *because*	**L&R**: Conversations about options for young adults	**W&S**: An interview with a partner about their interests
Lesson 4 Future with *will; want / would like* + object + infinitive	**L**: A conversation featuring problems and advice	**W&S**: Making suggestions about what to study based on things you know
Lesson 5 Questions with *why* and answers; conjunction *so*	**L**: A radio announcement	**S**: Talking about taking time off
	R: A paragraph about factors in planning for the future	
Lesson 1 *have to*	**R**: Job-hunting tips	**W&S**: Writing and discussing a to-do list
Lesson 2 *have to* and *must*	**R**: A to-do list	**W**: Help-wanted ads
Lesson 3 Comparative adjectives; *may* and *might*	**R**: Job postings	**W&S**: Preparing for and giving a job interview
Lesson 4 Superlative adjectives; *maybe, perhaps,* and *probably*	**R**: An announcement to students	**S**: Discussing factors in a decision that was made
Lesson 5 Intensifiers	**R**: An article about choosing a school	**S&W**: Making predictions
	R: A ratings table	**S**: Talking about feelings
	L&R: A conversation about studying abroad	**W**: Summary of a report
	L: A report on graduate programs	**S**: A grad school interview
Lesson 1 Phrasal verbs	**R**: Résumés and job applications	**W**: Filling out a job application
Lesson 2 *prefer* + noun, gerund, or infinitive	**L&R**: Invitation to an interview	**W&S**: Interviews and other communication between applicants and employers
Lesson 3 Advice with *should*, imperatives, and (*would*) *suggest/recommend* + gerund	**L&R**: A conversation about an interview	**W&S**: Describing job preferences
	R: A description of a bad interview	**W&S**: Giving interview advice
Lesson 4 *I know* + clause; conjunction *before*	**L&R**: The beginning of an interview	**W&S**: Guess which company!
		W: A presentation about a dream job
Lesson 5 Infinitives in common phrases	**L&R**: Job descriptions	**S**: Discussing potential jobs
Lesson 1 Object pronouns and reflexive pronouns	**R**: A short article introducing common job interview questions	**W&S**: Discussing, writing, and answering interview questions
Lesson 2 Simple past of *be; be like*	**R&L**: Descriptions of work experience and education in job interviews and cover letters	**W&S**: Describing job duties
Lesson 3 Simple past: regular verbs		**W&S**: Writing and talking about teamwork
Lesson 4 *when* clauses in past sentences; simple past: irregular verbs	**R**: A short article on how to approach difficult interview questions	**W**: Writing a cover letter
		W&S: Writing and talking about past experiences
Lesson 5 *when* clauses in future sentences	**R&L**: Wrapping up an interview	**W**: Long-term plans
	L&R: Job interviews	**W&S**: Job interview, ad, and description
	L&R: Job descriptions	

* Also, see the glossary in the back of the Workbook.

Contents

Grammar and Structures	Listening / Reading	Writing / Speaking
Lesson 1 Zero conditional **Lesson 2** Infinitives of purpose; *in order to* **Lesson 3** *be good/bad at*; *help* + object + (*to*) verb **Lesson 4** *would rather* **Lesson 5** *other* and *another*; *else*	**R** & **L**: An article about choosing majors **R**: Entries in a course catalog and other descriptions of courses **R** & **L**: Conversations about choosing and changing majors **R** & **L**: A conversation to report a decision **R**: An article about changing majors **L**: A report on popular majors	**W** & **S**: Discussing reasons for and factors in making decisions, especially related to studies **W** & **S**: Describing courses **S** & **W**: Asking for and giving advice and opinions **W** & **S**: Reporting on the past **W** & **S**: Describing what you and other people are good or bad at **S**: Describing preferences and persuading people **W**: An email describing feelings about school subjects
Lesson 1 adverbs of place **Lesson 2** *had better* (*not*) and *let's* **Lesson 3** First conditional; *have* + object + *to* verb **Lesson 4** *think* + (*that*) clause **Lesson 5** *keep/continue* + gerund; *why not* and *why don't*	**R**: A university brochure **R** & **L**: A conversation about changing schools **R**: Descriptions of students' problems **R**: A university's homepage **R** & **L**: A conversation about researching schools **R** & **L**: A conversation about studying abroad **R**: Descriptions of schools **L**: A report on graduation rates	**S**: Describing schools, including campuses and the surrounding area **S**: Discussing possibilities and decisions **S** & **W**: Asking for and giving information and advice **W** & **S**: Listing and discussing factors in choosing a school or university **S**: Discussing studying abroad **W** & **S**: Choosing a university **W** & **S**: Communicating at and about a school information fair
Lesson 1 Present perfect; *still*, *never*, and *yet* **Lesson 2** Simple past vs. present perfect; *few* and *a few*; *none* (*of*) **Lesson 3** Time expressions with the present perfect; empty *it* **Lesson 4** *ever*, *never*, and *always*; *while* and *during* **Lesson 5** *How long* questions with present perfect; *so far*	**R** & **L**: Taking time off **R**: An email about deciding to take time off from school **R** & **L**: Going home **R**: How to spend a vacation **R** & **L**: A part-time job **R**: A journal entry: video game **R** & **L**: Options for next semester **L**: An interview with an Advisor	**W** & **S**: A list of pros and cons **W** & **S**: Things you've done or would like to do **W**: Summarizing a problem and choosing from possible solutions **S**: Details about spending a break at home or on vacation **W** & **S**: Things you haven't done recently and how long it's been **W** & **S**: Asking questions to find out about people's travel goals **W** & **S**: Researching and discussing travel opportunities **S**: Discussing part-time jobs for college students
Lesson 1 *whether* and *if* **Lesson 2** Comparative and superlative adjectives: *more/most*, *less/least*; *both* A *and* B **Lesson 3** Comparing using *less*, *fewer*, and (*not*) *as… as…* **Lesson 4** *can* and *could* for possibility; phrases of agreement **Lesson 5** *either*, *neither*, and *both*; *too* and *enough* with adjectives	**R** & **L**: A conversation about studying abroad **L**: A study-abroad web page **L**: A description of a language school **R** & **L**: A conversation about studying abroad **R**: An online chat **L**: Conversations about choosing a country to study abroad in	**W** & **S**: Talking about decisions you need to make **W** & **S**: Rating your city **S**: Discussing which school to study at **W**: The best place to study **W** & **S**: Talking about study preferences **W** & **S**: Choosing the best city **W** & **S**: Opening a new language school

Module 1 Goals

Start a conversation

Discuss plans with other people

Link ideas with simple connectors (for example, *and*, *but*, or *because*)

Find the most important information in advertisements, information leaflets, web pages, etc.

Understand the main points in short, simple written news items and descriptions if you already know something about the subject

Understand the main information in news reports that you hear

Discuss different things to do, places to go, etc.

Briefly explain and give reasons for actions and plans if you have time to prepare

Preview

Look at pages 8 to 33. What pages are these things on?

-ed adjectives   _____

information about a career center   _____

an article about business schools   _____

a university ratings table   _____

Discuss

Talk about the questions with a partner.

1. What is happening in the photo?

2. What kinds of things might the woman be thinking about?

3. What is the best way to search for a job?

4. What are some challenges for young people today?

5. How does school help prepare people for the future?

Write

Choose one of the questions from above. Write a couple of sentences to answer it.

_____

_____

_____

Unit 1

Unit 2

Scan the QR code to watch a preview video.

Lesson 1	**What are your plans?**

A   Model Conversation

Listen to the interview. Then read the sentences. Listen again. Are the sentences true (t) or false (f)? 🔊 Track 02

1. _____ Phillip is thinking of going to college.
2. _____ Phillip is studying computer science.
3. _____ Sonya is working in Spain for six months.
4. _____ Sonya is traveling for six months.
5. _____ Yaser is going to apply to university.
6. _____ Yaser is working on his grandparents' farm.

For the false sentences, why are they false?

> **Brief note**
> To "think of" or about something means that you are considering it—that you might do it in the future.

B   Vocabulary

Listen to the interview again. Circle the words that you hear. 🔊 Track 02

gap year   run   volunteer   apply   student loan   experience   field   nanny

Now write each word next to the correct definition. Check your answers with a partner.

	a year between high school and college to travel, work, or rest		money that is borrowed from a bank to pay for school
	time spent doing something and the skills learned while doing it		to formally ask for something such as a job, usually in writing
	a person who helps parents with childcare		a subject of study or a kind of work
	to be the boss of; to direct or manage		to work/help people for no pay; a person who does this

C   Vocabulary Comprehension

Fill in the blanks with the correct words from part B.

1. Sonya is going to take care of children. She is going to work as a(n) _____.

2. Many students take a year off from studying before they go to college. They take a(n) _____.

3. Our store needs a new employee. You should _____ for the job.

4. I want to be a teacher, so I'm working as a volunteer at a school to get some _____.

D   Grammar

Brief note

Remember that you can use present continuous to talk about things happening at the moment of speaking. For example: *What **are you doing** right now? I'**m making** breakfast.*

Present continuous for future plans

subject	*be*	verb + *-ing* (+ object)	future time phrase
I	am	**starting** college	in September.
He / She / It	is	**visiting** Paris	next week.
You / We / They	are	**meeting** a friend	after school.
more future time phrases	soon, later, tonight, tomorrow, tomorrow morning / afternoon / evening, next Sunday, next weekend, in two hours / days / weeks / months / years		

Brief note

People do not always use time phrases. They use them when they want to be specific. These phrases usually come at the beginning or the end of a sentence.

E   Grammar Practice

Read each sentence. Write *P* next to sentences about the present and *F* next to sentences about the future.

1. _____ Please be quiet. I'm working on an assignment.

2. _____ My parents are having dinner at that new restaurant after work.

3. _____ He's doing research on local schools.

4. _____ Ahmed is waiting for the bus to take him home.

5. _____ Sarah and her sister are taking the train to London tomorrow.

6. _____ She is taking a shower at the moment.

Put the words in order to make sentences.

7. is / John / this / in / sister / his / visiting / Istanbul / weekend

   _____.

8. you / Saturday / are / what / doing / next

   _____?

9. boyfriend / next / getting / her / and / Jenny / year / married / are

   _____.

F   Use the Language

What are you up to?

Think about your plans for next month. Write them as notes. You don't have to write complete sentences.

> **My plans...**
>
>
>
>
>

Talk about your plans with a partner. Ask about your partner's plans. Do you have similar plans? When are you going to do these things? Are you and your partner busy?

When you are finished, talk with another pair about their plans. Then share with the class.

A Authentic Text: A career flyer

Read the flyer and answer the questions.

Brief note

The word "résumé" is often spelled *resume*. Another way to say *résumé* is *CV* (*curriculum vitae*, a Latin phrase).

Regular Activities

Coffee Time
Mon–Fri: 8:30 – 10:00 a.m.
• Meet new employees of the center

Job Fair
Last Thursday of every month
• Meet local employers looking for workers

Résumé Workshop
Third Wednesday of every month: 1:00 – 4:00 p.m.
• Develop your résumé with help from an expert

Career Center

Are you between the ages of 17 and 35? Looking for employment? Trying to decide what to do with your future? Drop by the Career Center and find out about the options available to you.
At the Career Center, you can:
• Start to think about your future
• Learn about career programs
• Get help with your résumé and practice job interview skills
• Learn about volunteering to help you get experience
• Search the job board
• Make an appointment with a career counselor
• Make new friends

Brief note

To drop by means to go to a place for a short time without an appointment.

1. Who can use the Career Center?

2. What happens every weekday morning?

3. How often is there a job fair?

4. When can you learn about writing cover letters?

5. How can you get in touch with the center?

Events this week

Rob Vega
Monday: 2:00 – 4:00 p.m.
• Government training programs

Annika Smith
Wednesday: 4:00 – 6:00 p.m.
• Writing a cover letter

Please register at the front desk.

Contact us

By phone: 204-555-6987   By email: info@cpc.edu   Like us on Facebook

B Vocabulary

Write each green word or phrase from part A next to the correct definition.

1. _____ from or around this area

2. _____ a meeting with someone at a specific time

3. _____ a face-to-face meeting to talk about a job

4. _____ a written list of your skills and experience

5. _____ to speak or write a message to someone

6. _____ an event where many employers meet people looking for jobs

7. _____ a letter about your experience

8. _____ the group of people who run a city, state, country, etc. and make laws

9. _____ work done for pay; a job, or the state of having a job

10. _____ a person who knows a lot about a subject

C About You

Discuss the questions with a partner.

1. Do you have a résumé? If you do, what do you have on it? If not, what can you write on one?

2. What are some local jobs or companies that you are interested in? Why?

D Grammar

Simple present vs. present continuous

Brief note

Stative verbs such as *love, own, want,* and *know* are not usually used with present continuous.

	simple present	present continuous
present meaning	things that are generally true; routines and habits	things happening at the time of speaking
examples	He **works** at the library. (He has a job at the library. Is he there right now? We don't know.) She **eats** lunch in the cafeteria. (This is her daily routine—she usually does it.)	He's **working** right now. (He's at his workplace and doing work.) She's **eating** lunch in the cafeteria. (It is lunchtime now, and she's eating in the cafeteria.)
time expressions	every day, week, month, morning, afternoon in the morning, afternoon, evening usually, often, never	right now at the moment
future meaning	scheduled actions on a timetable or calendar	plans
examples	My plane **leaves** at 6:45 tomorrow evening. Classes **start** on September 15.	I'm **meeting** Mom at the airport tonight. We're **seeing** a movie on Friday afternoon.

E Grammar Practice

Fill in the blanks with the correct form of the verbs.

1. My sister _____ (study) biology at university this year. She wants to become a doctor.

2. I usually _____ (walk) to school, but today I _____ (take) the bus because I _____ (be) late.

3. The teacher _____ (know) all of her students' names.

4. I _____ (eat) breakfast every morning—I _____ (need) it so I'm not hungry in class.

F Write to Speak

1. Write five questions you can ask someone about future plans. Use the time expressions below to help you.

next year	when you were a child	next week
after school	when you graduate	in five years

2. Now interview a partner about his or her future plans.

G Use the Language

Career counseling

With your partner, on a separate piece of paper, write a conversation between a career counselor and a person thinking about a new job. Talk about the person's experience, education, and skills. Try to decide on a good career for him or her. Then perform your conversation for the class.

A   Model Conversation

Read the conversation. Then listen. 🔊 Track 03

Elisa: Hey, Malak. You look really **worried**! What's the matter?

Malak: I decided to go to college next year, but I don't know what major to choose.

Elisa: Oh, that's a **tough** one. What do you like to do?

Malak: Well, I really enjoy being **outdoors**. I don't want an office job because I **can't stand** sitting down all day. But my parents think I should study **IT**. That's why I'm stressed.

Elisa: Hmm. I can understand that. But your parents can't make this kind of **decision** for you. What other things do you like doing?

Malak: I'm not sure. I need to think about that because my parents want to discuss my decision this week.

Elisa: The **recreation leader** program at the local college might be interesting. What do you think about that?

Malak: Sounds cool. I'll **look into** it. Thanks, Elisa.

> **Brief note**
>
> "IT" is an abbreviation of the phrase *information technology*.

B   Vocabulary

Write each bold word or phrase from part A next to the correct definition.

1. _____ hard

2. _____ outside

3. _____ to hate

4. _____ someone who leads activity groups (arts, sports, games, etc.)

5. _____ what a person chose; a choice

6. _____ thinking about problems and feeling stressed

7. _____ to try to get information about something

8. _____ the study of computers and how to use them to keep and communicate information

C   Vocabulary: Showing interest and understanding

Read the following expressions and their meanings.

a. What's the matter?	*What's wrong?*
b. That's a tough one.	*That's a hard problem.*
c. I (can) understand that.	*I see why you feel that way.*

Now listen to three people talk. Which expression should you use in each situation? Write the letter. 🔊 Track 04

1. _____   2. _____   3. _____

D Grammar

Gerunds and infinitives; conjunction *because*

verbs followed by gerunds (verb + -*ing*)	verbs followed by infinitives (*to* + verb)	verbs followed by both
enjoy finish quit dislike practice	learn need promise want decide	hate like love can't stand
I **enjoy** play**ing** piano. He **loves** listen**ing** to music.	She is **learn**ing **to swim**. We **want to go** downtown.	I **love to watch** TV in the morning. I **love listening** to the radio at night.

using *because* to give a reason	
because clause, clause (comma needed)	**Because** I like to watch TV at night, I often stay up too late.
clause + *because* clause (no comma needed)	I often stay up too late **because** I like to watch TV at night.

Brief note

A *clause* is a group of words with a subject and a verb.

E Grammar Practice

Find the errors in the sentences. Then rewrite them correctly. One sentence has two errors.

1. I enjoy to study English, because it will help me in the future.

   _____

2. She promised going shopping with me on the weekend.

   _____

3. My friend learned speak English by watching TV.

   _____

4. Because my brother can't play violin, we can't stand listen to him practice.

   _____

F Use the Language

What should they study?

Interview three of your classmates. Ask them about their hobbies and interests. Then suggest college majors for them. Fill in the chart with the information. (Note: If you have a major, don't say it. If you know a person's major, suggest a second major.)

When you are finished, discuss your ideas with each person. What do they think about your suggestions? Share your results with the class.

Person	Hobbies/Interests	Major

A   Model Conversation

Read the conversation. Then listen. 🔊 Track 05

Ahmed: Laura, congratulations! I heard you're going to medical school.

Laura: Thanks. Yeah, I found out yesterday.

Ahmed: Well, I'll call you when I'm sick.

Laura: I'll be a student for a long time. For the near future, you'll need to find another doctor.

Ahmed: You'll be great. I'm really happy for you. But I don't think I'll tell my mom about it.

Laura: Why not?

Ahmed: She'll be upset. She wants me to be a doctor, but I want to be a chef. I think I want to go to culinary school.

Laura: Do you know any good restaurants, then? Let's have dinner to celebrate.

B   Vocabulary

Listen to the words. Mark the stress in each word. Then practice saying them with a partner. 🔊 Track 06

architect – architecture

doctor – medicine

teacher – education

actor – theater arts

chef – culinary arts

carpenter – carpentry

Now say a sentence about each type of person and their field.

For example: *An **architect** works in the field of **architecture**.*

C   Grammar

Future with *will*

> **Brief note**
>
> In conversation, use the contracted form of *will* (*he'll, you'll,* etc.) and the negative form of *will not* (*I won't,* not *I'll not*).

using *will* to express future time: *will* + base verb	
possibilities	It's cloudy. I think it **will rain** this afternoon.
offers	The phone is ringing. I**'ll answer** it.
decisions made when speaking	That looks like a nice place to visit. Maybe we**'ll go** there next month.

want / would like + object + infinitive

	expressing preferences with *want / would like*
with a noun phrase	*Less formal*: I **want** <u>a cup of coffee</u>. *More formal*: I **would like** / I'**d like** <u>a cup of coffee</u> (please).
with an infinitive	*Less formal*: I **want** <u>to see</u> a movie tonight. *More formal*: I **would like** / I'**d like** <u>to see</u> a movie tonight.
with an object + infinitive	*Less formal*: My mother **wants** <u>me to go</u> medical school. *More formal*: I'**d like** <u>you to help</u> me with my résumé.

D Grammar Practice

Read the sentences with *will*. How is it used? Write *P* for a possibility, *O* for an offer, or *D* for a decision made when speaking.

1. _____ Please sit down. I'll bring you some water.

2. _____ That restaurant looks good. I'll book a table there tomorrow.

3. _____ The sky is very dark. I think it will rain this afternoon.

4. _____ That movie is really funny. You'll like it.

5. _____ That bag looks heavy. I'll carry it for you.

6. _____ That car is too expensive. Nobody will buy it.

Underline the errors and write the correct word(s) in the blank.

7. I'd like to eggs for breakfast, please. _____

8. My brother wants his friend helps him with his car. _____

9. She want to study film and television at college. _____

10. I'd would like my husband to cook dinner for me this weekend. _____

E Use the Language

Talking about people's plans

Choose one picture. Think about the person in it and write a few sentences about his or her plans and future dreams. What does the person want to do? What do you think he or she will do?

Read your sentences to a partner. He or she will try to guess which picture you're describing. Ask your partner why he or she thinks this. Is your partner correct?

A Model Conversation

Read the conversation. Then listen. 🔊 Track 07

Marco: Hi, Sophie. What's the matter? Why do you look upset?

Sophie: I'm not upset. I'm just tired of looking at these brochures from different colleges. I have to decide soon, so I'm researching a lot of schools and programs.

Marco: I'm ready for a break, too. I just finished cleaning up my house. I was dog-sitting for a friend, so there was hair everywhere! I'm tired of scrubbing and vacuuming. Let's get some coffee and complain.

Sophie: Coffee sounds great. I'll meet you at the coffee shop in half an hour.

Marco: All right, I'll see you then.

Listen to the conversation again. What is Sophie tired of?

_____

> **Brief note**
> The phrase "tired of" + noun/gerund means that you are bored or annoyed about something. You want to stop doing it.

B Vocabulary

Work with a partner. What are the people in the pictures doing? Write the correct words from the box.

vacuuming	ironing clothes	scrubbing	baking

1. _____   2. _____   3. _____   4. _____

Match the words with the correct definitions.

5. brochure •   • a. a rest or a vacation from work or school

6. break   •   • b. to get information about something

7. dog-sit •   • c. to care for someone else's dog for a short time

8. research •   • d. a small, thin book or magazine with pictures and information about a place, a business, etc.

C In Your World

What are three things you're tired of doing? Why? Ask a partner. Suggest what he or she can do instead.

> **Brief note**
> *Instead of..., you can...* is used to suggest a different action. For example: *Instead of doing the laundry, you can take your clothes to the dry cleaners.*

D Grammar

Questions with *why* and answers; conjunction *so*

asking for reasons with *why*	
question	answer
Why are you going to college?	**Because** I want to get a good job. I'm going to college **because** I want to get a good job.
	To get a good job. / I'm going to college **to get** a good job.
using *so*	
to give a reason	I'm going to college **so (that)** I can get a good job. Hugo gets up early in the morning **so (that)** he is not late for work.
to state a result	Kim was really late for work, **so** her boss got angry. I'm tired of studying, **so** I'm taking a short break.

Brief note

You can use *so that* to answer *why* questions, or you can use *so* without *that*.

E Grammar Practice

Write complete questions. Then answer them using *so*.

1. Q: Why / you / come / this school? → _____?

   A: _____

2. Q: Why / you / want / study / English? → _____?

   A: _____

3. Q: Why / people / want / learn / new languages? → _____?

   A: _____

F Listen to Speak

Listen to the conversation and answer the questions. 🔘 Track 08

1. What is Jared tired of? _____

2. What does Fatima suggest he do instead? _____

G Use the Language

Let's take a break!

Work with a partner. Take turns being Student A and Student B.

Student A

You are in your final year of school. You want to take a semester off, and you want your friend to take the semester off with you so that you can travel together. Explain to your friend why you want to take a break.

Student B

Your friend wants to take a semester off from school and wants you to take a break, too. You think this is a really bad idea, and you want your friend to stay in school and finish his or her studies. Tell your friend why taking a break is a bad idea.

A Radio Announcement

Listen to an announcement on a college radio station. Fill in the blanks with the missing information. 🔊 Track 09

- The ad is about _____.
- Only _____% of students use the college's Career Center.
- The Career Center is open from _____ to _____, six days a week.
- Volunteers can help with _____ and _____.

B **Write to Speak**

What are some questions you might ask a career counselor? Write them down.

_____

_____

_____

_____

C **Career Counseling**

Work with a partner. One of you will play a career counselor, and the other will play a student.

Career Counselor

You work in the Career Center at a large university. A student comes to you to discuss career options. Talk with the student. Find out what he or she is interested in. Then give the student some advice. Suggest at least two career options.

Student

You're a student at a large university. You go to see a career counselor to discuss your plans for the future. You don't know what you want to do, but your parents want you to be a teacher. You don't want to be a teacher. Ask the counselor for advice.

D **Reminder**

Some Module 1 Goals in Unit 1

Put a check mark (✓) next to the things you can do.

_____ Start a conversation

_____ Discuss plans with other people

_____ Briefly explain and give reasons for actions and plans if you have time to prepare

A Read to Write

Read the paragraph.

I'm finishing college soon. When I think about my future, two things are very important to me. The first is getting the right kind of job. I love art! I'm studying art history so that I can work in a museum. I want to keep studying art and help others learn about it. Second, I like helping people. I volunteer at a hospital, playing with sick kids and reading to them. I don't care about making a lot of money, so I don't want to work all the time. I'd like to have a lot of free time so that I can continue volunteering in the future.

B Prewrite

What's important to you?

When people make decisions about the future, they consider many different things. What is most important to you when you're making plans for the future? Read the list and add one item. Then number the items from 1 (very important) to 9 (not important).

_____ money

_____ time with family and friends

_____ becoming a better person

_____ being creative

_____ meeting new people

_____ helping people

_____ doing exciting things

_____ traveling

_____ education / learning new things

_____ _____
(your idea)

C Write to Speak

Write a few sentences describing what is important to you as you plan your future, what's not important, and why.

_____

_____

_____

_____

D Now Speak

Ask your partner what is most important to him or her when deciding a career. When you answer, do not read from your answers above. Compare your partner's answers to yours. Which are the same? Which are different? Give reasons for your decisions.

Then work together to create a new list. Compare the new list to the old lists. What changed?

Lesson 1   Searching for a Job

A   Authentic Text: A short article

Read the article from an employment website.

> **Brief note**
> A "tip" is a piece of advice or useful information.

Job-Hunting Tips

Looking for a job doesn't have to be frightening. You just have to have a good plan:

- Before you begin your job search, know your abilities and your goals for the position you want.
- Use employment websites and attend job fairs. Do research about a company before you apply for a job, and then send applications to companies you like.
- Make sure to clearly write your education, work experience, and volunteer positions in your résumé.
- When writing a cover letter, never sound boring! Try to sound interesting and ready to accept challenging duties. Then employers will want to hire you.
- You must have two or three references. These people can tell employers that you are hard-working, fascinating, and a good worker.

B   Vocabulary

Match the words with the correct definitions.

1. job hunting •
2. ability •
3. search •
4. accept •
5. duties •
6. reference •
7. position •
8. hire •
9. application •

- a. to look for (something); the act of looking for (something)
- b. a person who can give information about you and your experience
- c. to agree to do or have (something)
- d. the things you have to do in a job
- e. a skill; something a person is able to do
- f. to give (someone) a job
- g. a formal, usually written request for a job, admission to a school, etc.
- h. trying to get a job
- i. a specific job

C   Vocabulary: *-ing* adjectives

Circle the adjectives from the box in the article above. Then choose the correct answers.

> frightening
> interesting
> challenging
> boring
> hard-working
> fascinating

1. Which word means *very interesting*?
   a. boring   b. frightening   c. fascinating
2. Which word means *not interesting*?
   a. boring   b. frightening   c. fascinating
3. A person who is _____ accepts *challenging* duties.
   a. fascinating   b. hard-working   c. boring
4. Something *frightening* makes you feel _____.
   a. happy   b. tired   c. afraid

Grammar

have to

subject	(present tense) *have/has to*	verb + other information
I / You / We / They	**have to** **don't have to**	**accept** the position.
He / She / It	**has to** **doesn't have to**	**meet** a friend at the airport. **apply** for the job at the university.
subject	(past tense) *had to*	**read** this book before class.
I / You / We / They / He / She / It	**had to** **didn't have to**	**make** an appointment with the doctor.

Brief note

You can use *have got to* in the same way as *have to* in the present tense, but *have got to* has no past tense.

E **Grammar Practice**

Circle the correct answers.

1. You (has to / don't have to / had got to) be a great student to get a good job.
2. I didn't go to the party last night. I (have to / had to / don't have to) work on my résumé.
3. My sister has an exam tomorrow. She (has to / doesn't have to / have to) go to bed early.
4. As a kid, my father (has to / have to / had to) wake up early to work on his parents' farm.
5. I'm job hunting, and I (had to / has got to / have got to) send some applications today.

F **Read to Write**

Cassie wants a summer job at a clothing store. Here is a list of things she has to do to reach her goal. Read the list. Then answer the questions.

I have to…

✓ Finish writing my résumé. Include classes in fashion design and ability to give good fashion advice.

✓ Ask Mr. Brent, Mrs. Voss, and Prof. Nichols to be references.

✓ Do research on three stores.

✓ Complete applications and write a different cover letter for every store. In letters, write that I'm hard-working and will accept any part-time position.

1. What skills does Cassie have? _____
2. How many references does she want? _____
3. How many cover letters will she write? _____

G **Use the Language**

Job hunting

Think about a part-time job you would like to have. Write a list like the one in part F.

I have to…	Job: _____

Share your list with a partner. Does he or she have any tips for you?

21

A Authentic Text: A job poster

Read the job announcement and answer the questions below.

Office of the **Registrar** – Teaching Assistants Wanted

A Teaching **Assistant** (TA) helps a professor with lesson planning, lecturing, and grading. In this way, TAs get **valuable** experience in their field. All **applicants** must be students with an **excellent academic** history. The best applicants will be motivated, organized, and hard-working. They must be self-directed, and able to make decisions and solve problems.

Please **submit** the following **documents**: a cover letter, a completed résumé, three reference letters from professors, and a **transcript**. Interested students must submit these by August 1st. We will not accept applications after this date. We will contact **successful** applicants for an interview before August 15th.

1. Who can apply to be a TA? **2.** When is the deadline?

Brief note

The word *grade* is both a noun (an A, B, C, etc.) and a verb. As a verb, it means *to give a grade*.

B Vocabulary

Read the text again. Fill in the blanks with the correct bold word from the job poster.

1. A full list of a student's classes and grades is a(n) _____.
2. Another word for "very, very good" is _____.
3. Pieces of paper with important information on them are _____.
4. To give something (for example, a document or an assignment) to someone is to _____ it.
5. A person whose job is to help someone else is a(n) _____.
6. Someone who applies for a job is a(n) _____.
7. To do something well or correctly is to be _____.
8. A word to describe things related to school and studying is _____.
9. Something very useful or helpful is _____.
10. The person or office that keeps academic records is the _____.

C Vocabulary: *-ed* adjectives

In part A, circle the adjectives ending in *-ed*. These words describe how a person acts or feels. Then, in the chart, write the names of people you know with these qualities. Discuss your chart with a partner.

-ed adjective	This adjective describes...
motivated	
organized	
self-directed	

Which word best describes the woman in the picture? _____

have to and *must*

	have to + verb	*must* + verb
+	I **have to** find a job soon. (This is necessary.)	I **must** find a job soon. (This is necessary.)
-	You **don't have to** have a college degree to apply for this job. (It isn't necessary.)	Candidates **must not** submit applications late. (They cannot do this. It is a rule.)

E **Grammar Practice**

Read the letter and circle the correct words and phrases.

Dear students,

This year, the university has new rules to make our campus better for everyone. As of September:

1. Everyone (don't have to / must / must not) drive less than 40 km per hour on all campus roads. Those who don't follow this rule (must / have / must not) to pay $45 to the campus police department.

2. Smokers living in campus dormitories (must not / must / have to) smoke inside their buildings. There are smoking areas outside.

3. Students living in dormitories (must not / must / don't have to) leave the dorm during winter break. Students can stay in their rooms. But to do this, you (must / haven't got to / have) tell the housing office by Dec. 1.

4. All students and staff (must / have / don't have) to put garbage in trash cans around campus and in buildings.

Thank you,
Your Student Office

F **Write to Speak**

You are looking for a tutor to help you study and improve your grades. Write a description of your preferred candidate and make a list of rules your tutor must follow.

Tutor Wanted:

G **Use the Language**

Tutor Wanted

Write four or five questions to ask an applicant. Then find a partner and role-play an interview.

Is this candidate the right person for the job?

23

A   Authentic Text: A short article

Read the magazine article.

Choosing the Right Business School

Deciding on a business school can be difficult for future MBA students. To help our readers, *BusinessNews* wants to give you some information about schools in the Nortown area.

First, consider size. You might prefer a very large school such as Lakeshore University. You'll meet many different professors and have many classmates. Other students might like smaller class sizes. Uptown College may be better for these students.

Secondly, you may want a school with a great reputation in the field. Lakeshore has a better reputation.

Third, some MBA students may prefer a school with less expensive tuition. Fielding College is an excellent school, and it's cheaper than the other options.

Finally, some schools are more international than others. Interested in studying abroad for a semester? You might be happier at Wallborne Business School. It has larger international programs.

B   Vocabulary

Match the words with the correct definitions.

1. decide (on) •
2. quality •
3. location •
4. decision •
5. abroad •
6. reputation •
7. MBA •
8. course •

• a. a choice
• b. what people think about a person, place, etc.
• c. a class or a program of study
• d. a Master of Business Administration degree
• e. place; where something is
• f. to choose
• g. in another country
• h. how good or bad something is

C   Grammar

Comparative adjectives

> **Brief note**
> See Unit 8 to learn about comparison with *less*, *fewer*, and (*not*) as... as.

comparative adjectives			
one syllable adjective + *-er*	**adjectives ending in *-y*** *-y* to *-ier*	**two or more syllables** *more* + adjective	**irregular**
cheap – cheaper large – larger small – smaller	happy – happier pretty – prettier funny – funnier	more expensive more international more difficult	good – better bad – worse far – farther/further

Look back at part A. Underline seven comparative adjectives.

> **Brief note**
> To compare two people or things, you usually need *than*: *She's taller than him.*

may and might

<table>
<tr><td colspan="2">may + verb / might + verb</td></tr>
<tr><td colspan="2">These words give a possibility or prediction about the future.
When talking about possibility or prediction, may and might have the same meaning. They both mean there is a 50% chance.</td></tr>
<tr><td>may
might</td><td>They may go to a movie tonight.
She might apply for that teaching position.</td></tr>
<tr><td>may not
might not</td><td>I may not visit Sammy this afternoon.
Prof. Jenkins might not teach that course.</td></tr>
</table>

Brief note

A *prediction* is a guess about what will happen in the future.

Brief note

Don't use a contraction when you use *may* or *might* in the negative.

D Grammar Practice

Fill in the blanks with the comparative form of the correct adjective from the box.

specific	tough	far	heavy

1. Your course has more homework, but the tests for my course are _____.

2. Let me carry your suitcase. It's _____ than mine.

3. Ina's new apartment is nicer than her old one, but it's _____ from campus.

4. A: I'd like to take a class about animals.
   B: Hmm. Can you be _____? Which class?

Write your own sentences about what you *may / may not* and *might / might not* do this week.

5. _____

6. _____

7. _____

8. _____

E Use the Language

How did you decide?

Discuss with a partner how he or she decided to attend this school or program. Write an answer to the first question. Then mark each item on the list as important (I) or not important (N). Add items to the list if necessary.

My partner's decision

How did you find out about this school and program?

_____

Things to be considered:

_____ size of the school   _____ quality of the campus

_____ location of the school   _____ friends at the school

_____ quality of professors   _____ reputation of the school

_____ housing   _____ _____

_____ tuition fees   _____ _____

A Authentic Text: A ratings table

Read the table. Then answer the question below.

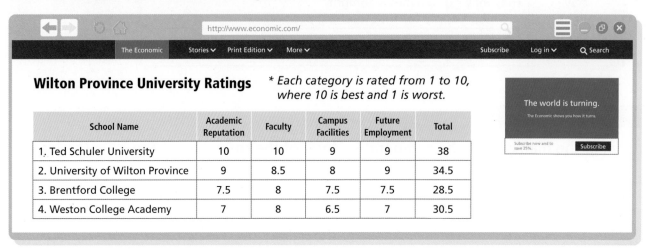

Wilton Province University Ratings * Each category is rated from 1 to 10, where 10 is best and 1 is worst.

School Name	Academic Reputation	Faculty	Campus Facilities	Future Employment	Total
1. Ted Schuler University	10	10	9	9	38
2. University of Wilton Province	9	8.5	8	9	34.5
3. Brentford College	7.5	8	7.5	7.5	28.5
4. Weston College Academy	7	8	6.5	7	30.5

What is the chart comparing?

a. All schools in a country   b. Universities in a province   c. The least expensive schools in a province

B Vocabulary

Choose the answer with the same meaning as the underlined word.

1. Ted Schuler University has the best <u>faculty</u>.
    a. students   b. teachers   c. textbooks   d. tuition

2. This chart does not <u>rate</u> class size.
    a. do research on   b. talk about   c. measure the quality of   d. experience

3. Weston College Academy has the lowest academic reputation in the <u>province</u>.
    a. state   b. country   c. city   d. field

4. The highest rating for campus <u>facilities</u> is 9.
    a. libraries and classrooms   b. sports centers   c. restaurants and dormitories   d. a, b, and c

5. These schools are rated on four <u>categories</u>.
    a. academic programs   b. cities   c. topics   d. employment

6. Weston College <u>Academy</u> has the lowest rating for campus facilities.
    a. museum   b. teaching   c. scholarship   d. school

C Grammar

Superlative adjectives

> **Brief note**
> See Unit 8 Lesson 2 to learn more about superlatives with *least*.

superlative adjectives			
one syllable adjective + *-est*	**adjectives ending in -y** *-y* to *-iest*	**two or more syllables** *most* + adjective	**irregular**
low – lowest high – highest	easy – easiest happy – happiest	worried – most worried beautiful – most beautiful	good – best bad – worst

maybe, perhaps, and probably

Brief note

Perhaps is formal; *maybe* is used much more often in spoken English.

50% probability or less	use *maybe* before subject	use *perhaps* before subject
	Maybe I'll apply to Harvard. **Maybe** he won't graduate this year.	**Perhaps** I'll apply to Harvard next autumn. **Perhaps** he won't graduate this year.
more than 50% probability	use *probably...*	
	after the main verb *be*: *He's **probably** a student.* before other main verbs: *They **probably** go to the university.* after a helping verb like *will* or *be*: *The subway will **probably** get him there fastest, so he's **probably** going by subway.* before a contraction with a helping verb + *not*: *They **probably** won't go to the same school. He's going to a local school, but she **probably** isn't.*	

D   Grammar Practice

Fill in the blanks with the superlative form of the adjective.

1. Sheri is the _____ (organized) person in our study group.

2. Which of these universities has the _____ (good) reputation?

3. The _____ (tall) building on campus is probably the library tower.

4. April is the _____ (rainy) month in my hometown.

Complete the sentences with *maybe*, *perhaps*, or *probably*.

5. It will _____ rain this afternoon. The forecast said there's a 60% chance of rain.

6. There might be a big storm tonight. _____ schools will be closed tomorrow.

7. Paul doesn't study, but he's the smartest person in class. He'll _____ get the best grade.

8. Ella has the least experience, but she's so hard-working. _____ that company will hire her.

E   Use the Language

Making predictions

Interview a partner. Ask for predictions about his or her future education and employment. Then take notes below. Where will your partner be next year, and what will he or she be doing? What about in two years? In five? Ten?

Next year	
In two years	
In five years	
In ten years	

On a separate piece of paper, write a few paragraphs about your partner's predictions.

A   Model Conversation

Brief note

"Definitely" means 100% probability.

Read the conversation. Then listen and answer the questions. 🔊 Track 10

Marta: I'm so excited about studying English abroad.

Cameron: Well, I'm jealous. I'd love to travel overseas.

Marta: You could come, too!

Cameron: Maybe. But I'll definitely have to wait until I save some money. So, where are you going?

Marta: I really want to go to England, but choosing a specific destination is pretty difficult.

Cameron: London would be fantastic. Lots of people, history, entertainment… Why not study there?

Marta: Well, it is a huge city with lots to see and do. But it might be too crowded for me. Living in a tiny rural area with friendly residents would be more my style.

Cameron: That sounds a bit boring. Maybe you could live in a bigger town near the sea.

Marta: Actually, I read about an English school located in a town called St. Ives. The shops, art galleries, and scenery looked quite nice in the brochure, and the school's teachers and homestay families seemed great.

Brief note

Here, "St." is short for, and is pronounced as, *Saint*.

1. Where does Marta want to go?   **2. What will she do there?**

B   Vocabulary

Fill in the blanks with the correct words from the box.

tiny	jealous	overseas	destination	entertainment
sea	residents	located	scenery	homestay

1. My best friend and I like the same kinds of _____—music, movies, and TV shows.

2. So, you're traveling _____? What's your _____?

3. My sister is so _____ of me. She always wants what I have.

4. Sao Paolo is a very large city _____ in Brazil.

5. I think Hawaii has the most beautiful _____ in the world.

6. To improve your English, consider living with a local _____ family.

7. She's from a _____ town—it only has about 400 _____.

8. It's nice to live near the _____. You can eat fresh fish all the time.

C   Quick Review

Look back at the brief notes in this module. What word or phrase means…

"100% probability"? _____

"bored or annoyed about"? _____ _____

"a guess about what will happen in the future"? _____

D   About You

What language do you want to learn? Where do you want to study abroad? Why?

E Grammar

Intensifiers

Brief note

When we use *quite* before a singular noun, *a* or *an* comes after it.

intensifier		after a linking verb	before a noun
mild	quite fairly rather	Vancouver is **quite beautiful**. Daniel is **fairly smart**. This music sounds **rather boring**.	Vancouver is **quite a beautiful city**. Daniel is a **fairly smart student**. This is a **rather boring song**.
strong	very really so such	The town isn't **very exciting**. The residents here are **really friendly**. Traveling overseas seems **so exciting!** X	The town isn't a **very exciting place**. There are really **friendly residents**. X This school has **such a good reputation**.
very strong	extremely completely totally	Sarah's course was **extremely difficult**. My friends feel **completely jealous**. This hike was **totally challenging**.	Sarah took an **extremely difficult course**. My friends are **completely jealous people**. This was a **totally challenging hike**.
Verbs often follow *really*. They can also follow *quite* and *rather*, but this use is formal.		She **really loves** her new job. They **rather enjoyed** the movie.	

Brief note

Don't use a noun after *so*, but always use one after *such*.

F Grammar Practice

Move the intensifier to the correct place in each sentence. Use an arrow (↓).

1. (such) Jeddah is a hot city.

2. (rather) This history lecture is interesting.

3. (so) The flight to Tokyo was long!

4. (quite) This is a good restaurant.

5. (really) Margaret is enjoying her English classes.

6. (very) The professors at this university are good.

7. (really) Scott loves his classes this semester.

8. (completely) We bought new furniture for the apartment.

G Use the Language

Talking about feelings

Look at the chart below. Think about a time when you felt the emotions and make notes about the situation. Then talk with a partner about your feelings and the situations when they happened. Make notes in the chart about your partner's experience.

	quite jealous	very excited	extremely angry	completely surprised
Me				
Partner				

Summary of a Report

Listen to the summary of a report on graduate programs. Fill in the blanks. 🎧 **Track 11**

1. The topic of the report is how _____

   _____.

2. The report used information from _____ schools over _____ years.

3. Today, applicants _____ have grades of 85% to 100%.

4. Many applicants must have work _____. For example, some worked as teaching _____.

5. Students applying to graduate programs usually need strong _____ from employers or _____.

6. In an interview, an applicant must show that he or she is interesting, _____, and _____.

Brief note

A *report* is a document giving information on a specific subject.

A Grad School Interview

Work with a partner. Discuss the questions.

1. Imagine you are applying to a graduate program. What subject will you study? What degree do you want? Tell your partner.

2. Using your partner's answers and the information from part A, write some interview questions to ask your partner.

3. Role-play the interview. Then switch roles.

Reminder

Some Module 1 Goals in Unit 2

Put a check mark (✓) next to the things you can do.

_____ Understand the main information in news reports that you hear

_____ Find the most important information in advertisements, information leaflets, web pages, etc.

_____ Understand the main points in short, simple written news items and descriptions if you already know something about the subject

Warm Up

Discuss the following questions in groups.

1. Do you have a part-time job now, or did you in the past? What do/did you do? Do/Did you like it or not?

2. What are some possible jobs that students might have on a university campus?

Job Ad

Read the job ad. With a partner, answer the questions. Would you like to have this job?

Position: International Student Assistant

Duties
As an international student assistant (ISA), you will help other international students at our university feel at home. Your duties are to greet new students when they arrive, show them around, and plan fun activities and entertainment for them.

Schedule
About 15 hours per week, mostly evenings and weekends

Applicants must:
- be current international students
- have a GPA of 3.0 or higher
- live on campus

No work experience necessary. Successful applicants should know the campus and the town well. They must be friendly, creative, and happy to help others.

To apply: Email your cover letter, résumé, and application form to isa@program.edu

1. Which of the following might an ISA do?

   a. Tutor students.   b. Help students apply to college.   c. Give students a tour of the city.

2. A successful applicant for the job does not have to _____.

   a. have good grades   b. have experience   c. work on weekends   d. submit a résumé

Help Wanted

Write an ad for a student job on campus. Include the following:

- Position name
- Main duties
- Work schedule
- Documents to submit
- Education and experience needed
- Skills needed

A Vocabulary

Remember and write...

1. ...five job titles.

_____ _____ _____ _____ _____

2. ...five things a person can study at college or university.

_____ _____ _____ _____ _____

3. ...three words beginning with *appl-*

_____ _____ _____

4. ...four activities people can be tired of doing at home.

_____ _____ _____ _____

5. ...three documents you might have to submit when applying for a job.

_____ _____ _____

6. ...four categories used to rate universities.

_____ _____ _____ _____

B Grammar

Underline the errors and write the correct word(s) in the blanks.

1. They are work on an assignment right now.   _____

2. He dislikes to listen to music.   _____

3. We won't having class next Monday.   _____

4. You aren't have to stand. You can sit here.   _____

5. Kate is tired of wash the dishes.   _____

6. They'll take probably a taxi.   _____

7. I was late for work, because my boss is angry at me. _____

8. Is your new job very challenged?   _____

9. Victor is so a nice guy.   _____

10. Would you like seeing a movie?   _____

11. She is a best doctor than him.   _____

12. It's cloudy this afternoon. I think it rains.   _____

C Planning

In a group, make plans to do something next week.

- Discuss what each person's plans are and what your schedules are like. Find a time that works for everyone.
- Talk about what activities and interests you each enjoy so you can agree on a fun activity.

D Success

Look at the list of adjectives. How important are they in helping people get a good job? Rate them from 1 (not important) to 10 (very important) and give a reason. Then find a partner and compare your lists.

	Rating (1-10)	Reason	Partner's rating
creative	_____	_____	_____
motivated	_____	_____	_____
organized	_____	_____	_____
self-directed	_____	_____	_____
fascinating	_____	_____	_____
beautiful	_____	_____	_____

E A Big Decision

Read the information about Ajay, a high school student in Canada. Then read the information about two colleges Ajay is considering.

Ajay

- From Canada
- Loves the sea and being outdoors
- Wants to be a doctor
- Can't stand big cities
- Likes small classes
- Would like to study abroad

UNIVERSITY OF MELBOURNE

- Located in a large city in Australia
- Medical school with a good reputation
- Around 40,000 students
- Many international students
- Fairly large class sizes
- Expensive for international students
- 20-minute drive to the sea

BISHOP'S UNIVERSITY

- Located in a medium-sized town in Canada
- No medical school, but good science programs and a good academic reputation
- Less than 5,000 students
- Small class sizes
- Reasonable prices; cheaper than other options
- Beautiful scenery, but 3 hours from the sea

Discuss Ajay's choices with a partner. Which school should he choose? Present your answer and your reasons to the class.

MODULE 2 Getting a Job

Module 2 Goals

Understand simple information and questions about work and hobbies

Talk to people politely in short social exchanges using everyday forms of greeting and address

Complete a questionnaire with information about your educational background, job, interests, and skills

Describe your education and your jobs, present and past

Make and accept invitations, or refuse invitations politely

Use the most important connecting words to tell a story (for example, *first*, *then*, *after*, and *later*)

Participate in a longer conversation about a familiar topic

Describe a job or a study experience

Preview

Look at pages 36 to 61. What pages are these things on?

Nicole Milton's résumé _____

a bad job interview _____

a cover letter _____

a timeline _____

Discuss

Talk about the questions with a partner.

1. How might the people in the picture feel? Why?

2. What is your dream job?

3. What should you wear to a job interview? Why?

4. What are some difficult questions to answer in an interview?

5. What should you do at the end of an interview?

Write

Choose one of the questions from above. Write a couple of sentences to answer it.

_____

_____

_____

Unit 3

Unit 4

Scan the QR code to watch a preview video.

Lesson 1 A Job Application

A Authentic Text: A job application

Ron wants to apply for a new job. Look at part of his résumé and then fill out the application.

Ron Lumber

1423 Bank Drive, Jackson,
MC, 34567 (555) 555-4536

Summary: I am looking for a permanent part-time position in administration.

Previous Employment:

Administrative Assistant
Hendrix Corp. (2 years)
78 John Street, Jackson,
MC (555) 555-9909

Please **fill in** the details.

Personal Data

Name: _____ Phone Number: _____
Address: _____

Position Information

Which kind of job do you prefer?
Hours (circle one): Part-time / Full-time
Type (circle one): Permanent / Temporary

> **Brief note**
> Use *fill out* to talk about the whole form, and "fill in" to talk about the individual blanks.

Previous Employment

Company Name: _____
Address: _____
Phone Number: _____
May we contact this employer? (circle one) Yes / No

B Vocabulary

Read each word. Then match the word with its definition. Check your answers with a partner.

1. administration
2. data
3. contact
4. hours

5. prefer
6. previous
7. qualification

8. Corp.
9. temporary
10. permanent

a. to like (something) better than something else
b. information
c. a short form of *corporation*, another word for company
d. a quality (degree, certificate) that makes someone able to do a specific job
e. in the past
f. lasting a specific amount of time
g. how much time a person spends working; the start and end times of a job
h. to get in touch with
i. activities related to running a company
j. for always; lasting an unlimited amount of time

C Vocabulary: Modals for permission

Many modals of possibility can be used to ask for permission—to ask someone about the possibility of being allowed to do something. Some sound more formal than others.

Less formal ⬇ More formal	**Can** we contact your past employer? **Could** I borrow your book, please? **May** we contact your past employer? **Might** I go to the washroom, please?

Practice reading the example sentences out loud. Then create more examples with a partner.

Grammar

Phrasal verbs

phrasal verbs		
Phrasal verbs are very common in conversation, but less common in writing. They are made up of a verb + particle—for example, *look up* or *fill in*. The particle is usually a preposition (*in, out, on, up, over,* etc.). But the meaning of a phrasal verb is not usually clear from the meaning of the verb and the preposition. You must study and remember the meaning of each phrasal verb. There are two kinds of phrasal verbs: inseparable and separable.		
Inseparable: The verb and the particle cannot be separated, so the object must come after the phrasal verb. Examples: *get on, get off, go over, drop by*	**get on:** board (a bus/train/plane)	You can't **get on** a plane without a ticket.
	go over: to review; to explain	Let's **go over** the meaning of each word.

Separable: The object *may* come between the verb and the particle. When the object is a personal pronoun, it *must* come between the verb and the particle.
Examples: fill out, fill in, look up, put on, throw out
    Get on <u>the bus</u> and take it to River street.
    ~~**Get** <u>the bus</u> **on** and take it to River street.~~
	fill out: to write information on a form	Please **fill out** this form.
		Please **fill** this form **out**.
		Please **fill** it **out**.
		(*X* Please fill out it.)

	look up: to find (information) in a dictionary, etc.	I **looked up** the word. I **looked** the word **up**. I **looked** it **up**. (*X* I looked up it.)

Grammar Practice

Circle the correct answers. Then read the sentences aloud.

1. He took an application and filled (out it / it out).

2. Fill (in / up) your name and phone number, please.

3. I need to get (on / in) the train and go five stops.

4. You should look (out / up) that company to learn more about it.

5. This milk doesn't smell good. I'm going to throw (it out / out it).

6. Where are my shoes? I want to put (on them / them on).

7. Would you drop (over / by) my office after lunch?

8. Please go (over / out) your information before submitting the form.

Write to Speak

1. Go online and find some more phrasal verbs. Write them down here, with their meanings.

2. With a partner, write a conversation between a job applicant and an employer. Try to use a few phrasal verbs. Remember that the job applicant should be polite when speaking to the employer.

3. When you finish writing your dialogue, practice it with your partner. Switch roles and practice again. Then perform it in front of the class.

A   Model Conversation

Read the conversation. Then listen. Track 12

Ben: Hello. May I speak to Mariana Gonzales, please?

Mariana: This is Mariana.

Ben: Hello, Mariana. My name is Ben King, and I'm calling from Jackson Industries. We went over your application for employment, and we'd like to invite you to come in for an interview.

Mariana: Wonderful! Thank you very much.

Ben: You're welcome. We advertised two positions: one in administration and one in human resources. Which one would you prefer to interview for?

Mariana: I think I'd like the administration position.

Ben: Great. We think your strengths suit that position as well. When would you prefer to come for an interview? I can meet you at any time on Thursday or Friday.

Mariana: I'd prefer to do the interview before noon on Thursday if possible.

Ben: How's Thursday at 10 a.m.?

Mariana: Sounds great. I look forward to meeting you.

B   Vocabulary

Match the words with the correct definitions.

1. human resources •
2. noon •
3. appreciate •
4. strength •
5. preference •
6. administrative •
7. look forward to •
8. suit •

• **a.** 12:00 p.m.
• **b.** to match
• **c.** an ability; a skill
• **d.** to be happy about something that will happen
• **e.** to feel thankful
• **f.** relating to running a business
• **g.** the part of a business involving hiring
• **h.** a thing someone likes more than another

C   About You

What are your biggest strengths as a current or future employee? In a job interview, which of your skills or abilities would you prefer to talk about? Write a few sentences. Then discuss them with a partner.

Grammar

prefer + noun, gerund, or infinitive

prefer + noun, gerund, or infinitive		
The verb *prefer* can be followed by a noun, a gerund, or an infinitive. There is no difference in meaning.		
***prefer* + noun**	***prefer* + gerund**	***prefer* + infinitive**
I **prefer the bus.** She **prefers a morning appointment.** We **prefer recent graduates.**	I **prefer taking** the bus. She **prefers making** a morning appointment. We **prefer hiring** recent graduates.	I **prefer to take** the bus. I **prefer not to drive.** Would you **prefer to meet** on Thursday or Friday? I'd **prefer to meet** on Thursday.

E
Grammar Practice

Put the words in order to make sentences.

1. contacting / prefer / directly / they / applicants

   _____.

2. he / prefers / morning / in / coffee / the

   _____.

3. applicants / they / tomorrow / would / call / prefer / to

   _____.

4. she / not / to / by / prefers / subway / go

   _____.

5. would / here / you / prefer / to / sit / or / there

   _____?

6. prefer / I'd / not / to / work / that / company / for

   _____.

F
Use the Language

What kind of job do you prefer?

Read the chart with questions about job preferences. Circle your answer and give a reason. Then add two more questions, answer them, and give reasons.

Would you prefer...	Reason:
to work indoors or outdoors?	
a younger boss or an older boss?	
to work alone or in a team?	
a small company or a big company?	

Now find a partner and discuss your answers.

Brief note

A   Model Conversation

We say "Guess what." to introduce information that could be surprising.

Read the conversation. Then listen. Track 13

Demar: Hey Jenny, guess what. I have a job interview tomorrow!

Jenny: Oh, congratulations!

Demar: Yeah, but I'm a bit nervous. Do you have any advice for me?

Jenny: Well, you should research the company before an interview. You should also ask a few questions toward the end. That shows you're really interested in the job.

Demar: Should I bring an extra copy of my résumé?

Jenny: That's a good idea. I'd also suggest arriving early. And choose your outfit carefully—first impressions are important.

Demar: Thanks for the tips, Jenny.

Jenny: One more thing—don't forget to get plenty of sleep the night before.

Brief note

The words "suggest" and *recommend* are very close in meaning. They are both used to give advice.

B   Vocabulary

Match the words in the box with the correct definitions.

1. outfit •
2. first impression •
3. arrive •
4. recommend •
5. a bit •
6. forget •
7. plenty •
8. confirm •

• **a.** a lot; enough or more than enough
• **b.** an opinion of someone after your first meeting
• **c.** to say that something is good; to suggest
• **d.** to get to a place; to come
• **e.** to make definite
• **f.** a little
• **g.** to not remember
• **h.** all the clothes a person is wearing at one time

C   Vocabulary Comprehension

Fill in the blanks with the correct words and phrases from part B.

1. I _____ checking your résumé carefully before submitting it.

2. It's okay to feel _____ _____ stressed before an interview. Most people do!

3. You can usually find _____ of information about a company online.

4. You don't have to wear expensive clothes to a job interview, but wear a nice _____.

5. Be sure to _____ the address of the company before you go to the interview.

6. Always be on time. Never _____ late to an interview!

7. When you meet an employer, it's important to make a good _____ _____.

8. Don't _____ to say thank you at the end of the interview.

Now check your answers with a partner and read the sentences out loud.

Grammar

Advice with *should*, imperatives, and *(would) suggest/recommend* + gerund

You should + verb…	imperatives	(would) suggest/recommend + gerund
You **should ask** a few questions. You **should wear** a nice outfit to an interview.	**Don't forget** to get plenty of sleep the night before the interview. **Research** the job before you go.	I **suggest reading** about it online. I **would recommend arriving** early. I**'d suggest** researching the company.
Should is polite and can be used between friends and coworkers.	Imperatives are less polite and have a strong meaning.	*Suggest* and *recommend* are formal and used often in writing or polite speech.

> **Brief note**
>
> *I would (I'd) suggest…* has the same meaning *as I suggest…*, but is a little more formal and polite. This is also true for *I would (I'd) recommend*.

E **Grammar Practice**

Underline the errors and write the correct word(s) in the blank.

1. You should sending a thank-you email after the interview. _____
2. I suggest call to confirm the interview time. _____
3. Being ready to answer questions about your previous jobs. _____
4. You should bringing a copy of your résumé with you. _____
5. I recommend to practice interview questions with a friend. _____
6. I suggest read about the interviewer online. _____

F **Use the Language**

A bad interview

Read Bryan's request for advice after a bad interview. Discuss his problems with a partner. Then respond to Bryan's letter by giving him some advice for his next interview.

Dear _____,

I'm so upset. I had an interview yesterday, but I didn't get the job. I arrived a bit late because I couldn't find the office! Then, when I got into the room, I didn't know how to answer the interviewer's questions. I didn't know what questions to ask, either. She told me at the end of the interview that I didn't get the job. How can I do better next time?

Dear Bryan,

_____

_____

_____

_____

_____

A Model Conversation

Read the conversation. Then listen. Track 14

Vanessa: Thank you for coming in today. Your résumé is outstanding. Let's talk about the position. First of all, what do you know about our company?

Julian: I know Jon Benny established it ten years ago, and now it supplies paper to a lot of companies around the country.

Vanessa: That's right. I know you have a lot of experience selling paper, so that could be very helpful to us. Next, I want to ask you: Why did you decide to leave Paul's Paper?

Julian: Well, I hope to have a long career in the industry. I didn't think that Paul's Paper could give me that. I know that Benny's Paper Supply offers professional development. That sounds really interesting to me.

Vanessa: Yes, we do. Okay, let's talk about some of the details of the position.

B Vocabulary

Listen to each word. Then write each word next to the correct definition. Track 15

| helpful | outstanding | supply | professional development | establish | hope |

1. very good; excellent   _____
2. learning more job skills   _____
3. to start (something, like a company)   _____
4. to want something to happen and think that it will happen _____
5. making it easier to do something; giving help   _____
6. to give; to offer   _____

> **Brief note**
> As an adverb of sequence, *then* is not followed by a comma.

C Vocabulary: Adverbs of sequence

An adverb often describes a verb (an action), but an adverb of sequence can describe a whole sentence or idea. You can use adverbs of sequence to talk about the sequence (or the order) of things that happen.

First (of all),	Second, (Third, etc.)	Next, / After that, / Then	Finally, / Last, / Lastly,

Imagine that your friend has an important job interview tomorrow morning. You are giving him or her advice about getting ready for the interview. What should he or she do, and in what order? Write a few sentences.

D Grammar

I know + clause; conjunction *before*

sentences with *I know*	
Use *I know* (*that*) + clause to talk about things you know.	
I know (that) he established the company ten years ago.	**I know (that)** you have a lot of experience selling paper.
using *before* to express time	
A conjunction connects two parts of a sentence. Conjunctions often show the relationship between these two parts. Use the conjunction *before* + clause to show time order: one thing happens at an earlier time than another. The conjunction *before* can come before or after another clause. The clause with *before* talks about what happens later. The other clause tells what happens earlier.	
Before we start, I'd like to tell you about the position.	I'd like to tell you about the position **before** we start.

> **Brief note**
>
> Use a comma to separate two clauses when the sentence begins with *before*.

E Grammar Practice

Fill in the blanks with the correct words or phrases from part D.

1. I researched the company _____ I went to the interview.

2. _____ we begin, we need to go over your résumé.

3. _____ this company needs to improve its business soon.

4. I know _____ your company offers professional development.

5. First of all, I _____ that your employees are very happy here.

6. _____ I came to work here, I worked for three years at a similar corporation.

F Write to Speak

Go online and research two companies. They can be from your country or from another place. Try to choose companies that the rest of your classmates will know. Fill in the table with as much information as you can.

Company 1	Company 2
Name:	Name:
City and country:	City and country:
Date established:	Date established:
Products they sell:	Products they sell:
Other information:	Other information:

G Use the Language

Guess which company!

Describe one of the companies from part **F** to your partner using the information in the chart. Do not say the name of the company. Your partner can try and guess the name of the company.

Play the game again with another partner. Then share your results with the class. Did your partner guess correctly? Can your classmates guess the companies?

A   Model conversation

Read the conversation. Then listen. 🎧 Track 16

Donna: You're interviewing to be a graphic designer here. Let me give you a **job description** for that position.

Logan: Please.

Donna: You'll be **in charge of** a **project**, and you'll need to know the **client** very well. Our **department head**, Robert, can explain the project to you. You will also need to know the **brand** you'll be working with. Are you **familiar with** brand research?

Logan: Yes, definitely.

Donna: Great. In order to get you started as soon as possible, you need to schedule meetings with your project team members. You'll need to work **closely** with them at the beginning.

Logan: Great. I'm looking forward to it.

B   Vocabulary

Fill in the blanks with the correct bold words or phrases from part A.

1. Mina worked at a hospital, so she's _____ _____ the medical field.

2. For the best possible result, it's important to work _____ with your team members.

3. This is an exciting _____ to work on!

4. The _____ _____ lists the graphic designer's duties.

5. Coca-Cola is an example of a famous _____.

6. I'm a career counselor, and I try to help every _____ find a good job.

7. The _____ _____ manages the whole team.

8. At a restaurant, the chef is _____ _____ _____ the kitchen.

C   Vocabulary: Other job titles

Look at the list of job titles and the brief description of each.

art director	a person in charge of the schedule of illustrators and designers
project manager	a person in charge of planning and completing projects
content developer	a person who writes content for a website
web designer	a person who designs a website
marketing supervisor	a person who supervises people who work in advertising
communications director	a person who works with the media (TV, newspapers, social media)

Which of these jobs are you interested in? Why? Discuss your answers with a partner.

_____

D Grammar

Brief note

Use *be able to* instead of *can* after another modal verb.
(✓) You must be able to...
(X) You must can...

Infinitives in common phrases

infinitives in common phrases		
phrase	**meaning**	**example**
need to + verb	must do something	You'll **need to work** closely with them at the beginning.
be able to + verb	can do something	You must **be able to work** on current projects.
know how to + verb	have knowledge of the way to do something	You'll need to **know how to work** on a team.
in order to + verb	with the purpose of doing something	**In order to get** started as soon as possible,...

Brief note

See Unit 5 Lesson 2 to learn more about *in order to*.

E Grammar Practice

Circle the correct answers.

1. He is able to (do / doing) many projects at the same time.
2. Do you know how to (write / writes) a job description?
3. I need (to develop / develop) a new website for our company.
4. Let's hire someone else in order to (work / works) faster.
5. New employees should (can / be able to) ask questions.
6. We need to (scheduling / schedule) a meeting as soon as possible.
7. Department heads must know how (to teach / teaching) their employees.
8. Ben researched the company (in order / be able) to do well at his interview.

F Use the Language

My dream job

Think of a job you would love to have—your "dream job." Go online and research what skills you need for this job. Take notes below and prepare a short presentation about it. Explain to the class the skills and experience needed for your dream job. Which skills and experience do you already have? What do you need to learn? What qualifications do you need? Is it a popular or common job in your country? Be sure to give as many details as you can.

Notes:
know how to...
be able to...

You can begin your presentation with:

I'd like to talk about my dream job. My dream job is _____.

A Nicole's Résumé

Read the résumé.

Nicole Milton

2345 Avenue Road, Big City, MD, 98987 / (999) 555 – 3456

Summary: I am an administrative professional looking for a permanent, full-time position at a company.

Work Experience

Administrative Assistant, Highbrow Corp., 2013-2017
- Provided administrative help to the management department
- Assisted the human resources department in hiring
- Answered telephone calls and e-mails

Assistant to the Creative Director, Moviebox Corp., 2011-2013
- Scheduled appointments and gave other administrative help to the creative director
- Brought new clients to the company and worked closely with them

Volunteer, Central City Children's Hospital, 2010-2011
- Assisted doctors and nurses
- Ran activities for children and their families

Education

B.A. in Business Administration, North College, 2011
Graduated from Jackson High School, 2007

B Prepare

Write possible answers to some interview questions about Nicole's résumé.

1. Are you able to work well with members of an administrative team? _____

2. Why did you leave the Highbrow Corporation? _____

3. Do you know how to schedule meetings? Do you have experience with this?

   _____

C Nicole's Interview

Role-play a conversation between Nicole and an interviewer. Use the résumé to help you ask and answer questions.

D Reminder

Some Module 2 Goals in Unit 3

Put a check mark (✓) next to the things you can do.

_____ Complete a questionnaire with information about your educational background, job, interests, and skills

_____ Use the most important connecting words to tell a story (for example, *first*, *then*, *after*, and *later*)

_____ Describe a job or a study experience

Read to Speak

Read the job description.

Company: ANNEX Corporation	
Position Title: Communications Director	
In this job, you will need to:	**We offer:**
• be able to work alone or as part of a team • participate in professional development programs • establish new relationships with clients • work on more than one project at the same time	• a flexible schedule • professional development • a part-time or full-time schedule • an office located near public transportation

B **Listen to Speak**

Listen to a phone call and answer the questions. 🔵 **Track 17**

1. Why is the woman calling Tom?

   _____

2. What company does she work for?

   _____

3. What did the woman receive from Tom?

   _____

4. What position did Tom apply for?

   _____

5. What does Tom think about his skills and the position?

   _____.

6. What day and time is Tom's interview?

   _____.

C **Write to Speak**

Choose a partner to role-play a conversation. Choose roles and make notes to prepare for your conversation.

Role: Applicant

You have an interview for this communications director position. You want to tell your friend about it. Give details from the job description and the conversation in part B. Ask your friend for interview advice.

Role: Friend on the phone

Your friend calls you with some good news—he or she has a job interview soon! Ask your friend some questions about the position, and give him or her some tips for the interview.

D **Now Speak**

Role-play your conversation. When you finish, switch roles and have the same conversation.

In which role did you speak more fluently and easily? Why?

Lesson 1 · Basic Questions

A · Authentic Text: A short article

Read the article about common job interview questions. Then discuss the questions below with a partner.

Looking for a new job is easy. Interviewing for a job and actually getting it are the hard parts. In particular, job interviews can be stressful and difficult to prepare for. In order to do better in an interview, it's important to prepare yourself for questions that will probably come up. You don't have to memorize your answers, but thinking about possible questions and how to respond will help a lot. Here are the top ten interview questions that you should prepare for:

1. Tell me about yourself.
2. What did you like or dislike about your old job?
3. What challenges and problems did you face?
4. What was your biggest accomplishment in your old position?
5. What is your biggest strength? Your biggest weakness?
6. Why did you leave your previous job?
7. Why should we hire you for this position?
8. What are your future goals?
9. Why do you want to work for us?
10. Are you willing to relocate?

Which of these questions do you think is the easiest to answer? Which is the hardest? Why?

B · Vocabulary

Fill in the blanks with the correct words from the box.

willing	come up	challenge	accomplishment	weakness
respond	memorize	face	prepare	relocate

1. We didn't talk about Nick's new job at dinner. The topic didn't _____ _____.

2. I decided not to take the job because I didn't want to _____ to a new city.

3. People living in cities _____ different problems than people living in the country.

4. I have one big _____ as an employee: I'm not very good at talking in front of groups.

5. Graduating from college is an important _____.

6. I sent Salena an email yesterday, but she didn't _____.

7. One _____ for college freshmen is cooking for themselves.

8. Before a job interview, you should _____ one or two questions for the interviewer.

9. How can we _____ all these vocabulary words by tomorrow?

10. Mika is a nice person. She's always _____ to help.

C · About You

Discuss these questions with a partner. Then share your answers with another pair.

Would you consider moving abroad for a job? Why or why not? Where would you want to go? Why? What's the biggest accomplishment of your life so far? Why is that your biggest accomplishment?

Grammar

Object pronouns and reflexive pronouns

object pronouns and reflexive pronouns							
Object pronouns take the place of the noun that is the object of the verb or preposition.							
I → **me**	you → **you**	he → **him**	she → **her**	it → **it**	we → **us**	they → **them**	
Joe was angry at his <u>sister</u>. → Joe was angry at **her**.				I introduced <u>Joe</u>. → I **introduced** him.			
Reflexive pronouns are used when the subject and the object (of the verb or preposition) are the same. *Joe was angry at <u>Joe</u>. Joe was angry at **himself**. (Don't say Joe was angry at Joe.)*							
I → **myself**	you → **yourself**	he → **himself**	she → **herself**	it → **itself**	we → **ourselves**	you → **yourselves**	they → **themselves**
Please introduce **yourself**. Marisa cooks for **herself**. We take care of **ourselves**. David doesn't like to talk about **himself**. I wrote a story about **myself**.							

Grammar Practice

Circle the correct answers.

1. Nice to meet (you / yourself). Tell me a little about (you / yourself).
2. I need to speak to Julie. Will you please call (her / herself)?
3. Mia said hello to the professor and introduced (her / herself).
4. We really appreciate Kevin and Martin's help. How can we thank (them / themselves)?
5. Ricardo saw Mr. Gibbs and asked (him / himself) about the job.
6. I could see (me / myself) in the window.
7. Yana is sleeping. Try not to wake (her / herself) up.
8. My brother loves selfies. He always takes pictures of (him / himself) with his phone.

Use the Language

Choosing interview questions

Imagine you are an employer and you will soon interview someone for a job. Choose the kind of job and write down five interview questions. They can be easy or a little difficult, but try to ask *wh-* questions, not yes/no questions.

> Job: _____
>
> 1. _____
> 2. _____
> 3. _____
> 4. _____
> 5. _____

Choose a partner and interview him or her. Then answer your partner's questions.

Compare your questions with your partner's. Did any questions surprise you? Which questions were the hardest to answer? Which were the easiest?

A Model Conversation

Read the conversation. Then listen. (Track 18)

Interviewer: You were a writer for a fashion magazine. **Describe** that job. What was it like?

Ines: It was a great **entry-level** position. I learned a lot about fashion. I had to do a lot of research about current **trends** and **come up with** ideas for articles.

Interviewer: Sounds interesting. How many people were there on your team?

Ines: There were eight of us. Everyone had a different **background**. But that wasn't a problem. They were all very **easygoing** and **encouraging**.

Interviewer: That's great. Were there any challenges while working there?

Ines: There weren't a lot of challenges. But if I had to name one, it would probably be the long hours. Some days we had to work a lot of **overtime** in order to meet a **deadline**.

Interviewer: That can be tough. But it seems like you liked the job. What did you enjoy most about it?

Ines: I enjoyed the **teamwork**. I was also happy to get experience and develop my creative writing skills.

B Vocabulary

Write each bold word or phrase from part A next to the correct definition.

1. _____ showing someone support
2. _____ to think of (an idea or plan)
3. _____ extra time at work
4. _____ relaxed and informal
5. _____ a person's past, experience, education, etc.
6. _____ at the lowest level of a job or career
7. _____ things that are currently popular
8. _____ working with others to reach a goal
9. _____ to tell someone about (something or someone)
10. _____ the time when something (a project, assignment, etc.) must be finished

C In Your World

Think about your last job or think of an imaginary one. What were some things that you had to do? Make a list of some of your duties. Then ask your partner about some duties that he or she had and make another list. Are any of the duties the same?

Your answers
- _____
- _____
- _____
- _____
- _____

Your partner's answers
- _____
- _____
- _____
- _____
- _____

D Grammar

Simple past *of be*; *be like*

simple past of *be*		
The past tense of *be* has two forms: *was* and *were*.		
statements	questions	negatives
I / He / She / It **was**… We / You / They **were**…	**Was** I / he / she / it…? **Were** we / you / they…?	I / He / She / It **was not**… We / You / They **were not**…
It **was** a great entry-level position. There **were** eight of us.	What **was** it like? How many people **were** there on your team?	But that **wasn't** a problem. There **weren't** a lot of challenges.
You can use *there was* or *there were* to make statements or ask about something in the past. When a sentence begins with *there*, the subject comes after *be: There were apples.* In questions, *there* follows *was* or *were: Were there any apples? How many apples were there?*		
questions with *be like*		
You can use questions with *be like* to ask someone to describe something. These questions have the form *What + be* verb + subject + *like?*		
What **is** your teacher **like**? What **were** your coworkers **like**? What **was** your previous job **like**?		

E Grammar Practice

Underline the errors and write the correct word(s) in the blank.

1. I were the only one who watched the movie. _____

2. We was planning to visit our grandparents last week. _____

3. There was many people in the park yesterday. _____

4. There were a strange car parked in front of my house. _____

5. In your previous job, what your team was like? _____

6. Was there any messages left for me? _____

F Use the Language

Teamwork

Think about times when you worked as part of a team at school or at work. How was working with a team different from working alone? List some of the pros (positive things) and cons (negative things) about teamwork.

Pros	Cons

Did you list more pros or more cons? Share your answers with the class.

A   Model Conversation

Read the conversation. Then listen. 🎧 Track 19

Interviewer: Could you please describe your education?

Ari: Sure. I graduated two years ago with a B.A. Then last year, I got a certificate in project management at another college. I thought I should have some more practical skills.

Interviewer: What is your degree in?

Ari: English literature. And I minored in history. I love learning about past societies.

Interviewer: Did your studies benefit you in your last position?

Ari: Yes, I think so. I wrote a lot of company correspondence, so I needed good writing skills. I also managed the planning phase of many projects, so my certificate was useful.

Interviewer: And what did you learn from your previous position?

Ari: I realized that teamwork is more than just working together. It's also about understanding the other team members' strengths and weaknesses.

B   Vocabulary

Match each of the words from the box to a definition below.

a. correspondence	b. certificate	c. benefit	d. manage
e. society	f. useful	g. phase	h. realize

1. to direct or be in charge of   ____
2. a large group of people living in a community   ____
3. letters and e-mails   ____
4. to help or to have a good effect on   ____
5. to begin to know or understand   ____
6. helping you to do something; helpful   ____
7. a document showing that you have a skill   ____
8. a part of a process   ____

C   In Your World

Use some of the past time expressions and simple past verbs below to write true sentences about yourself. Then compare your sentences with a partner's.

A few years ago…	I realized…
Last week…	I managed…
Last summer…	I learned…
A couple of months ago…	I graduated…

Brief note

Past time expressions usually come at the beginning or the end of a sentence.

_____

_____

_____

Simple past: regular verbs

simple past: regular verbs	
To form the simple past of a regular verb, add -(e)d to the end of the verb. learn → learned realize → realized graduate → graduated	
Sometimes the spelling changes.	
When the word ends in -y, change -y to -i and add -ed.	copy → copied study → studied
When there is a single stressed vowel before a single final consonant, double the final consonant and add -ed.	stop → stopped plan → planned

Brief note

Do not double x, w, or y: fix → fixed; allow → allowed; annoy → annoyed.

E **Grammar Practice**

Fill in the blanks with the correct forms of the given words.

1. I _____ working at that company a few years ago. (stop)

2. She _____ me last night about the project. (call)

3. We _____ together at a coffee shop last summer. (work)

4. Leah _____ in art history in college. (major)

5. Then I _____ that I didn't have my wallet. (realize)

6. My roommate _____ some chicken for dinner last night. (fry)

7. I _____ my vacation in Mexico last summer. (enjoy)

8. Henry _____ to go on a short trip. (prefer)

9. Paula _____ this department for ten years. (manage)

10. I _____ that graduating from college was important. (decide)

F **Read to Write: A cover Letter**

Brief note

You can begin a letter with "Dear Sir or Madam" when you do not know the name of the person who will read it.

Read about what a typical cover letter should include.

Parts of a cover letter

JOHN DOE

📱 +1 234 567 890   🌐 www.johndoe.com
✉ johndoe@johndoe.com   Ⓢ socialsite/johndoe

JOHNDOE
GRAPHIC DESIGNER

DEAR SIR, MADAM

I. Contact information: This is the first part of your cover letter. You should include your name, address, phone number, and e-mail address.

II. Greeting: You should address the person you are contacting. Follow your greeting with a comma. For example: *Dear Mr. Jones, ...*

III. Body: The body says what position you are applying for and why the company should choose you for an interview. It also suggests scheduling an interview.

   A. 1st paragraph: Tells the reader why you are writing the letter. Try to get the interest of the reader and say what position you are applying for.

   B. 2nd paragraph: Says what you can offer the company. Describe your previous work, skills, and accomplishments.

   C. 3rd paragraph: This is your closing. Summarize what you can bring to the company and suggest the next step by requesting a meeting or phone call.

Sincerely,

John Doe

Look up example cover letters on the Internet. Then, on a separate piece of paper, try writing your own cover letter.

A   Authentic Text: A short article

Read the article. Then listen. Track 20

Tips on Interviewing

Your job interview is tomorrow, and you're a bit anxious. You wonder what questions the interviewer will ask. Unfortunately, there may be some difficult questions. The interviewer might ask about your biggest strength and biggest weakness, why you left your previous job, or how you are different from other applicants. Thinking about and practicing your answers to these questions will help give you confidence.

There are also some things you should not do at an interview. First, don't lie! Be honest about your experience and education. Second, don't ask about salary or say what salary you're seeking. Wait for the interviewer to bring up that topic. Finally, do not say bad things about your previous job. Employers don't want to hire a person with a negative attitude.

B   Vocabulary

Read the conversation again. Match the words to the correct definitions.

1. confidence   •
2. salary   •
3. lie   •
4. wonder   •
5. seek   •
6. unfortunately •
7. bring up   •
8. attitude   •

- **a.** to say something that is not true
- **b.** to look or ask for
- **c.** a feeling that you can do something well or succeed at something
- **d.** how much money an employee gets for his or her work
- **e.** a word meaning that something is bad or unlucky
- **f.** to begin to talk about (a topic)
- **g.** to think and guess about something that you do not know
- **h.** the way that you think or feel about something or someone

C   About You

What are three of your strengths and three of your weaknesses? Discuss them with a partner.

D   Grammar

when clauses in past sentences

Brief note

Use a comma between clauses when the *when* clause comes at the beginning of the sentence.

when clauses in past sentences
You can use *when* clauses in statements and questions to talk about a specific time in the past. *When* is followed by a clause to give a time: *when* + clause (subject + verb). The *when* clause must appear with another clause in the same sentence.
What was your biggest weakness **when you were at your last job**?   **When a great company offered my husband a position,** we decided to relocate.

Simple past: irregular verbs

simple past: irregular verbs
Irregular verbs in the simple past do not end in -(e)d. You have to memorize these verb forms.

| drink → **drank** | eat → **ate** | feel → **felt** | get → **got** | have → **had** | leave → **left** |
| read → **read** | see → **saw** | take → **took** | think → **thought** | wake → **woke** | write → **wrote** |

E   **Grammar Practice**

Circle the correct answers.

1. I (drink / drank) too much coffee last night. I didn't sleep well.

2. We (see / saw) a really boring movie last week—*The Researchers*.

3. What time will you probably (leave / left) tonight?

4. Pablo (thinks / thought) the class was boring, but I enjoyed it.

5. Willy (read / readed) hundreds of books before he turned nine years old.

Put the words in order to make sentences.

6. was / when / called / Paolo, / I / asleep / he

   _____.

7. did / started / you / where / it / raining / go / when

   _____?

8. was / nervous / met / Lana / when / interviewer, / she / the

   _____.

9. Oliver / happy / when / was / the / got / job / he

   _____.

F   **Listen to Speak**

Listen to part of an interview and take notes. Then answer the questions. ⏺ Track 21

Notes:	

- What question did the interviewer ask the woman first?
- What was the woman's response?
- What question did the interviewer ask the woman next, and how did the woman respond?
- What two reasons did the woman give for leaving her last job?

G   **Use the Language**

Let's talk about the past.

Cut or tear a piece of paper into eight smaller pieces. On each piece, write the base form of an irregular verb. Then, with your partner, mix up your pieces of paper. Take turns choosing a word and using it to talk about your past. You can talk about anything, but you have to use the word. Your partner should ask questions about what you say. Try to give as many details as possible.

A Model Conversation

Read the conversation. Then listen. Track 22

Interviewer: Where do you see yourself in five years?

Anna: Well, when I find a permanent position, I'll **work on** becoming a manager. I hope to run my own **department someday**.

Interviewer: That's great. We're looking for someone **long-term**. Well, that's it for today. Before we **wrap up**, do you have any other questions about the position?

Anna: No, I can't come up with anything at the moment. Wait. Actually, yes. What is the **starting date** for this position?

Interviewer: Oh. The starting date is on the first of next month, so in about three weeks. When we finish interviewing all the **candidates**, we'll make a decision, and you'll **hear from** us by the end of the week.

Anna: Sounds good.

Interviewer: Excellent. I'll be in touch, Anna. Thank you.

Anna: Thank you very much. Goodbye.

B Vocabulary

Write each bold word or phrase from part A next to the correct definition.

1. _____ to finish or end something
2. _____ a job applicant
3. _____ to spend time trying to do or improve something
4. _____ the day when something begins
5. _____ relating to or happening over a long period of time
6. _____ at some time in the future
7. _____ a part of a company dealing with specific duties
8. _____ to get a call, email, etc., from someone; to receive communication from someone

C Vocabulary: Future time expressions

Study the time expressions. Then work with a partner. Take turns making sentences using the expressions.

- in two years
- someday
- in about five weeks
- (by) next day, week, month, year
- tonight, tomorrow, the day after tomorrow
- next season (spring, summer, fall, winter)

D About You

Imagine yourself in five years. What will you do? Where will you live? Write a few sentences about your five-year plan. Then discuss it with a partner.

Grammar

when clauses in future sentences

when clauses in future sentences
You use *when* + clause in future statements and questions to talk about a time in the future when something happens. The *when* clause uses the simple present tense, not the future. It can come first or second in the sentence.
When I find a permanent position, I'm going to work on becoming a manager. (**Not** ~~When I'll find...~~) = I'm going to work on becoming a manager **when I find a permanent position.** **When we finish interviewing all the candidates,** we will make a decision. (**Not** ~~When we will finish...~~) = We will make a decision **when we finish interviewing all the candidates.**

Brief note
Use a comma only when the *when* clause comes first.

Grammar Practice

Write correct, or underline the errors and write the correct word(s) in the blank.

1. When I have a permanent position, I'm going to buy a house. _____

2. What will you do when you will finish school? _____

3. When he's getting the promotion, he'll be very happy. _____

4. I'll call you when I arrive at the office. _____

5. What will happen when you're finishing the interview? _____

6. When you'll finish the project, you will be able to relax. _____

7. What are you going to do when you graduate? _____

Quick Review

Look back at the brief notes in this module.

1. Circle the correct words: You fill (in / out) information in order to fill (in / out) a form.

2. What is another word for suggest? _____

3. How do you start a letter if you don't know the name of the person?
   Dear _____ *or* _____, ...

4. How can you bring up information that might be surprising? _____ _____.

Use the Language

Long-term plans

On a separate piece of paper, draw a timeline like the one below. Write as many future events in your life as you can think of. Try to be specific about when they will happen.

When you are finished, find a partner. Look at your partner's timeline and ask them questions about the events.

Listen to the interview. Fill in the blanks with the missing words. Then practice the interview with a partner. Change roles and practice again. ⊙ Track 23

Interviewer: It's nice to finally meet you, James. Thank you for coming in for the interview.

James: It's great to meet you, too. I'm a bit _____, but I'm very excited about this _____. When I _____ last year, I wanted to work for this company.

Interviewer: That's great to hear. You certainly seem like an excellent _____ for this position. I see on your résumé you have many _____ _____. What did you major in _____ you were at school?

James: I _____ in computer science. I taught _____ a lot about computers when I was in high school, but I learned a lot in college, too.

Interviewer: Well, the position we have is _____-_____. It is a position with _____-_____ opportunities. The _____ is always growing, so we're opening up new offices in several locations.

James: That sounds interesting.

Interviewer: If we decided to hire you, would you mind _____ to a new area?

James: No, I wouldn't mind that at all.

Interviewer: Great. Can you tell me a little more about _____?

James: Well, I enjoy _____, and I can deal with _____ situations very well.

Interviewer: That all sounds great. When we _____ _____ the interviews, I will be _____ _____. Take care, James.

James: Thank you. You too.

Write a summary of James's interview on a separate piece of paper. What is some key information about James? Compare your summary with your partner's.

Then role-play a conversation between James and the interviewer. The interviewer calls to offer James the job, and James accepts. Discuss the starting date and other details about the job. Then switch roles.

Some Module 2 Goals in Unit 4

Put a check mark (✓) next to the things you can do.

_____ Understand simple information and questions about work and hobbies

_____ Talk to people politely in short social exchanges using everyday forms of greeting and address

_____ Describe your education and your jobs, present and past

_____ Participate in a longer conversation about a familiar topic

Read the following job descriptions.

STORE MANAGER NEEDED

Full-time position—40 hours a week
Required qualifications and experience:

- At least 2 years of management experience
- A bachelor's degree in business
- Excellent communication skills

Please contact Jeff at 555-6868 or send your résumé to jeffjohns@admin.net

FASHION DESIGNERS WANTED!

Full-time position—30 hours a week
Required qualifications and experience:

- A degree in fashion, art, or design
- A love of fashion
- Excellent communication skills
- No experience necessary!

Please send your résumé to fashqueen@fashion.net

Think of a job and create an advertisement for it.

Position: _____

Required qualifications & experience: _____

_____

_____

Contact information: _____

_____

_____

Work with a partner. Choose the role of interviewee or interviewer.

Role 1: Interviewee

Choose one of the jobs from above. Tell your partner which job you chose. Prepare for any questions an interviewer might ask a candidate for this job. Then answer your partner's questions politely, professionally, and to the best of your ability.

Role 2: Interviewer

You will interview your partner for the job he or she chose. Prepare questions about the candidate's education, work experience, etc., and then perform the interview politely, professionally, and to the best of your ability.

When you finish, switch roles. Try to play your new role without looking at any notes.

A Vocabulary

Complete the crossword.

Across →

3. to be ___ with = to know about
4. the opposite of strength
7. The project is in the planning ___.
9. someone who buys a service
10. excellent
12. to get (something) ready
13. to start (a company, etc.)

Down ↓

1. Try to make a good first ___.
2. to say something false
5. to look for
6. I ___ who that woman is. Do you know?
7. a lot; enough
8. ___ your apartment. What is it like?
9. I'm calling to ___ our appointment for 3:00.
11. Apple is a popular computer ___.

B Grammar

Fill in the blanks.

1. I was tired, so I went to bed early and _____ for nine hours!

2. The bus stopped, and we got _____.

3. What _____ your old job _____? _____ you enjoy it?

4. There _____ ten people at the meeting yesterday.

5. Nice to meet _____. Tell me about _____.

6. I _____ from college four years _____.

7. Do you want my advice? I _____ talking to a career counselor.

8. Erica went to college _____ order to study nursing.

9. _____ of all, let's talk about your experience.

10. After we wrap _____ the meeting, let's go out for coffee.

11. I'll contact you _____ we finish all the interviews.

12. Would you prefer _____ sit inside or outside?

Find an example résumé online for a person seeking a job in a field that interests you. Discuss it with your partner. What skills and education does the person have? What else does the résumé include?

D Prepare for an Interview

You have an interview for a great job tomorrow morning, and you want to be prepared. Fill in the table with a few notes on what you should do and say.

What to wear	
Good words to describe myself	
Accomplishments to bring up	
Strengths and skills to talk about	
Questions to ask the interviewer	

Now read some difficult questions interviewers often ask. Try to think of four more difficult questions. When you're done, practice asking and answering these questions with a partner.

Common difficult interview questions:	Your own difficult questions:
What are your strengths and weaknesses?	•
Why did you leave your previous position?	•
How are you different from other candidates?	•
How much you are seeking in salary?	•

E Group Interview

Work in a group of three to four people. Choose one of the photos below. On a separate piece of paper, write the job interview that you imagine is happening. Then role-play the conversation.

Changes at School

Module 3 Goals

Ask and answer simple questions about school, likes, and dislikes

Understand short, simple texts containing familiar vocabulary, including
international words

Explain why you like or dislike something

Write about yourself (for example, information about your school) using simple
language

Describe plans and alternatives

Describe past activities, events, and personal experiences

Ask and answer simple questions about things in the past

Understand the main points in short newspaper or magazine stories

Preview

Look at pages 64 to 89. What pages are these things on?

the inside of a modern home _____

a man writing a letter to his family _____

a list of university majors _____

two women talking on a subway _____

Discuss

Talk about the questions with a partner.

1. What do you like about being a student? What do you dislike?

2. What would you like other people to know about you?

3. What are you planning to study soon?

4. What is something interesting that you studied?

5. What did you try to learn that was difficult?

Write

Choose one of the questions from above. Write a couple of sentences to answer it.

_____

_____

_____

Unit 5

Unit 6

Scan the QR code to watch a preview video.

Lesson 1	Deciding What to Study

A Authentic Text: A short article

Read the article. Then listen. 🎧 Track 24

Students Face Challenges When Choosing Majors

For many students today, the most difficult decision is not whether to go to college—it's what to study when they get there. If a student becomes unhappy after choosing a major, that

▲ University of Glasgow

student has another difficult decision to make: "Should I stay in my current program, or should I spend more time and money to start again?"

Changing majors is quite common, but it can be difficult. If you want to avoid this situation, it's best to ask yourself some important questions before making a choice. What are your interests? Does a specific major offer good career opportunities? Which major is more difficult or competitive? And, finally, which factor is most important to you? If you ask yourself these questions and answer honestly, you can avoid more difficult, more expensive decisions later.

B Vocabulary

Fill in the blanks with the correct words from the box.

situation	interest	factor	avoid	opportunities	program	competitive	offer

1. It's hard to get into Harvards Business School. It's very _____.
2. I want to get scholarships to pay for college so that I can _____ loans.
3. Violin is a popular _____ at the Juilliard School.
4. Does your university _____ a degree in cosmetology?
5. I like design, but my real _____ is architecture.
6. It is a terrible _____ if you graduate college but still can't find a job.
7. Tuition was the most important _____ in my decision to study at Bismarck State College.
8. If you have a degree in nursing, there are many job _____ for you at hospitals in the city.

C In Your World

Look at the list of factors to consider when choosing a major. Add one of your own. Then rank the factors in order from most important (1) to least important (5). Talk with a partner about the reasons for your choices.

- _____ Personal interest
- _____ Career opportunities
- _____ Difficulty
- _____ Competitiveness
- _____ Other: _____

Grammar

Zero conditional

zero conditional	
A zero conditional sentence is an *if* sentence that expresses something generally true. It has an *if* clause (expressing a condition) and result clause. Both clauses are in the simple present tense.	
if clause	result clause
If plants don't get water,	they die.
If you have a degree in nursing,	you have many job opportunities.
If you mix blue and yellow,	you make green.
If the weather is good,	students like sitting in the quad.

Grammar Practice

Match the two columns to make sentences.

1. If students don't study hard, •
2. If you go to a lecture, •
3. You have to think carefully •
4. If you major in English literature, •
5. If the weather is really bad, •
6. Do you go to your dorm room •

• **a.** if you want to change your major.
• **b.** does your university cancel classes?
• **c.** if you need a quiet place to study?
• **d.** they don't do well on their exams.
• **e.** you should arrive on time.
• **f.** you have to read Shakespeare.

Complete the sentences with information that is true for you. Use an *if* clause or a result clause.

7. _____, I study all night.

8. I feel really nervous _____.

9. _____ if I don't eat lunch.

10. If I have to make a big decision, _____.

Use the Language

A big decision

Imagine you're planning to change your major, have a gap year, or even quit school. Think of some reasons to do one of those things and make notes.

Which are you planning to do?

_____

Why? _____

_____

_____

_____

Change majors?
Take a break?
Quit school?

Now discuss your situation with a partner and ask for advice.

A   Authentic Text: A course catalogue

Read the catalogue.

Hampshire State University Majors

We offer the following short descriptions to give students basic information about the majors in our undergraduate program. If a specific major interests you, please contact the related academic department to learn more.

Political Science: Study the history and theory of politics in order to better understand governments and how they work.

Philosophy: Review and explore 3,000 years of human ideas in order to understand our world and the meanings of life.

Linguistics: Learn about the languages of the world, including their histories, similarities, and differences.

HAMPSHIRE
STATE

B   Vocabulary

Fill in the blanks with the correct words from the box.

theory	assist	professions	politics	advertising
products	relations	similarities	social	

1. International _____:

    Study how different countries work together, and why they sometimes don't. Students in this major learn about the relationships between the world's countries, especially their _____ and differences in _____ and economics.

2. _____:

    Understand different ways to sell _____ and services. Students will also study _____ in order to learn the major ideas of the business.

3. _____ Work:

    Prepare for _____ in hospitals and government offices. Students will learn to _____ people in need of help.

C   About You

Discuss the following questions with a partner. As you talk, make notes about some of your answers.

1. What did you learn in high school? _____

2. What didn't you learn enough about? _____

3. What should you learn? _____

Now discuss how these things affected (or are affecting) your choice of a university major.

Grammar

Infinitives of purpose; *in order to*

infinitives of purpose	
usage	examples
An infinitive (*to* + verb) often states the purpose of an action.	They went to Yale **to study political science**. **To improve your grades**, you should study every day.
In order to is another common way to express purpose. It sounds a bit more formal.	They went to Yale **in order to study political science**. **In order to improve your grades**, you should study every day.
In order not to is the correct way to express a negative purpose.	**In order not to wake up my roommate**, I left the apartment quietly.
The infinitive phrase (*to* + verb) can be put at the beginning of a sentence, followed by a comma, or it can go last with no comma before it.	

Grammar Practice

Fill in the blanks with the correct phrases from the box. Add commas where necessary.

to pay tuition this semester	in order to think about my future	in order not to fail the test

1. I decided to take a year off _____.

2. _____ I applied for a student loan.

3. _____ I will study until midnight every night this week.

Now write three sentences about what you did last week. Use infinitives of purpose to say why you did these things.

_____

_____

_____

Use the Language

Describing a major

Choose a university major to write about. It could be your major or just one you are interested in. Write a short description of the major. Then, with a partner, discuss the majors you each wrote about.

Name of Major: _____

Short Description: _____

_____

_____

A   Model Conversation

Read the conversation. Then listen. 🔊 Track 25

Akio: I want to change majors. I think I made a mistake when I chose medicine. Help me decide on a subject.

Sloan: What are you good at?

Akio: I'm good at science; I just don't like it. I want to study something I'm good at—but something I like.

Sloan: So what else are you good at?

Akio: I'm good at speaking, I think. Arguing... I'm good at persuading people, and I like discussing ideas.

Sloan: Then what about something like law?

Akio: No, thank you! I don't want to spend hours studying boring legal texts. I want to motivate people and help them work well together, but I don't want to spend a lot of time arguing details of the law.

Sloan: Maybe you should think about business—advertising or management. You could even work at a medical company. Then you could use your knowledge and your passion!

> **Brief note**
> In this conversation, "else" means something different from medicine. What is a *different* major he's good at? See Lesson 5 to learn more about *else*.

B   Vocabulary

Write the words next to the correct definitions.

detail	knowledge	passion	argue
persuade	motivate	spend	legal

1. _____ to get someone to think or act in a specific way
2. _____ to give an opinion with reasons
3. _____ what you know
4. _____ to make someone want to do something
5. _____ to use time or money for something
6. _____ related to the law
7. _____ a strong feeling
8. _____ a small point

C   In Your World

With a partner, write down a few school or university subjects. What can motivate people to study these subjects? Then discuss careers these subjects can prepare you for.

Subjects	Reasons to Study	Related Careers

Grammar

be good/bad at; help + object + (*to*) verb

be good/bad at + noun	*be good/bad at* + gerund	*help* + object + (*to*) verb
She **is good at math**. He**'s bad at photography**. I**'m** not very **good at music**.	She **is good at solving** math problems. He**'s bad at taking** photographs. I**'m** not very **good at singing**.	My brother **helped me to choose** my major. Nobody **helped them pay** their tuition. Please **help her find** the athletic center.

Brief note

To be *good/bad at* something means that you do it well/badly.

Brief note

It's more common to leave out the *to* than to include it in sentences with *help* + object + (*to*) verb.

Grammar Practice

Put the words in order to make sentences.

1. very / cooking / good / am / at / I / not

   _____.

2. professor / understand / my / me / helped / history / the war

   _____.

3. my / at / bad / laws / is / professor / explaining

   _____.

4. friends / her / major / helped / her / a / choose / to

   _____.

5. us / help / our / you / project / finish / can

   _____.

Speak to Write

Look at the images below. What might these people be good at? What should they major in? What careers should they try? Compare your ideas with a partner's.

Use the Language

What are you good at?

On a separate piece of paper, write a short paragraph about something you're good at—not something related to your major. How did you become good at it? How could you use this skill in the future?

Share your paragraph with a partner.

A Model Conversation

Read the conversation. Then listen. 🔊 Track 26

Asefeh: I have to choose my major by the end of this semester, and I still don't know what's best for me.

Troy: Aren't you doing well in your math classes?

Asefeh: I am, but I do better in engineering.

Troy: Then, you should study engineering. You'd be able to get a really good job after college.

Asefeh: It sounds like a good idea, but I'm not sure. Would I rather study mechanical engineering or computer science?

Troy: Computer science? Are you thinking of that too?

Asefeh: Yeah. I had to do some programming for my laboratory work. I learned it quickly, and I really liked it. But if I choose that, I have to study for another semester to catch up with the students in the computer science department.

B Vocabulary: Some majors

Write the majors under the correct pictures.

| travel and tourism | forestry | African-American history | programming |
| finance | graphic design | hospitality management | interior design |

a. _____

b. _____

c. _____

d. _____

e. _____

f. _____

g. _____

h. _____

C About You

Look at the majors in part B and answer the following questions. Discuss your answers and reasons for them with a partner.

Which of these majors...

1. ...would you be good at? Why?

2. ...would you be bad at? Why?

3. ...would you like the best? Why?

would rather

	would rather + verb	
comparing two options	*would rather* + verb... + *than*...	I **would rather write** an essay **than** take a test. He'**d rather study** Latin **than** Greek.
questions	*Would* S *rather* + verb... + *or*...?	**Would** you **rather go** to the museum **or** see a play?
using context	We can use *would rather* with only one option when we know the other option.	A: Do you want to eat in the dining hall? B: No, I'**d rather eat** off campus.
would rather not	S *would rather not* + verb.	We **would rather not attend** a lecture early in the morning. (= We don't want to...)

Brief note

With personal pronouns, the short form of would (*'d*) is often used.

Fill in the blanks with the correct words from the box.

or	would	rather	not	than

1. She's changing her major because she _____ rather learn chemistry.

2. I think I'd rather take a break for one semester _____ study this fall.

3. Would you _____ get the easiest job or the one that pays best?

4. Would they rather give their presentation this Tuesday _____ Wednesday?

5. I would rather _____ go to an expensive university.

Would you rather...?

Work together in groups of two to four students. Write several *Would you rather*...? questions. Offer two good choices or two bad choices, and ask your classmates to choose. You can use the pictures below for ideas.

_____
_____
_____
_____
_____
_____

A Model Conversation

Read the conversation. Then listen. Track 27

Mom: I'm glad you like your new roommate. What else is happening with you?

Jeremy: Actually, I have some big news about school. I **finally** made the decision to **switch** to another major—from psychology to music **therapy**.

Mom: What?

Jeremy: I know. It's surprising, right?

Mom: Why the change? You chose psychology as a major two years ago. I thought you wanted to be a counselor. Isn't music just a hobby?

Jeremy: I'm interested in both counseling and music. And they're **related**—both are ways to get people to express themselves. But music therapists can get jobs more easily than psych majors, so it's a **practical** choice.

Mom: Jeremy…

Jeremy: And their work often pays better. But most importantly, I love music. That can motivate me to work harder at becoming a great music therapist.

Mom: I guess… if it's something you love, you should do it.

Jeremy: You don't seem happy about this, but it's **generous** of you to **support** me anyway. **Trust** me—this is a good choice.

> **Brief note**
> The subject psychology is often shortened to "psych" in informal conversation.

B Vocabulary: Feelings

Write each bold word or phrase from part A next to the correct definition.

1. _____ having a relationship; connected
2. _____ to change from one to another
3. _____ giving a lot; being very helpful
4. _____ in the end; after a long time
5. _____ really useful; in a way that considers results
6. _____ to believe that someone is honest or correct
7. _____ help for a person who is sick or has a problem
8. _____ to say or show that you agree with someone or something

C Quick Review

Fill in the table with the correct forms of each adverb.

Adverb	easily	well	hard	_____	_____
Comparative	more easily	_____	_____	more importantly	_____
Superlative	most easily	best	_____	_____	earliest

D About You

Talk to a partner about things you do well and things you'd like to do better. How could you do them better?

E Grammar

other and another; else

other and another	else
Other is often used with plural nouns. *Another* is only used with singular nouns.	*Else* is used after the question words *how, what, where, who,* and *why* to mean "more," "other," or "different."
At our company, M.B.A. graduates earn more than **other** employees. I want to move out of my room and go to **another** dormitory.	What **else** is new with you? A: Katie is coming to the party. B: Good. Who **else** is coming? I don't like this table. Where **else** can we sit?

F Grammar Practice

Fill in the blanks with *other*, *another*, or *else*.

1. I'm studying literature this semester, but I may switch to _____ major.

2. I know you're good at math. What _____ are you good at?

3. Cristina knows all the _____ people in her yoga class.

4. Who _____ is graduating next semester?

5. I need _____ pen—this one isn't working.

6. Our university has a bigger business library than _____ schools.

7. Would you like _____ cup of coffee?

8. Are there any _____ international students in our department?

9. Practicing a foreign language is hard, but how _____ can you learn?

G Use the Language

Writing home

Write a short email to a friend or family member to tell him or her about a school subject that you don't like. Explain why, and then explain what you'd like to study instead.

_____

_____

_____

_____

_____

_____

_____

A A Short Article

Read the article and answer the questions.

More Students Changing Majors

College students change their majors more often now than they did in the past. You may be surprised when you find out how often: in America today, 80% of students change their major once or more. A deeper look into the trend should persuade us to worry less when a friend or family member plans to change majors.

Students generally change majors for positive reasons. A student rarely changes majors just because he or she is unhappy. Changes are most common after a student finds another subject he or she likes more. Students often switch majors when they take an interesting elective and find out they are very good at it. They discover a new talent that makes them feel better about themselves.

"I was afraid to change my major, but now I know it's common. I'm not the only one."

The decision to change majors isn't easy, and it can be expensive. But even when many people around the country are worried about money, students change majors because they would rather study an interesting subject than one with better job opportunities. Responding to a recent survey, the most popular reason students gave for changing majors was "to avoid starting a career that will make me unhappy later in life." Parents may worry about their children losing opportunities for better jobs after graduation, but future happiness is also important.

1. What do students do more today than they did in the past? _____
2. What is a common reason for changing majors? _____
3. How do some students find out what they are really good at? _____

B Discussion

Discuss the following questions with two or three other students.

1. What do you think about changing majors?
2. Do you think it's okay for a student to switch majors three or more times?
3. What would you say to friends, family, or a professor to explain why you want to change your major? Role-play this conversation with your partners.

C Reminder

Some Module 3 Goals in Unit 5

Put a check mark (✓) next to the things you can do.

_____ Ask and answer simple questions about school, likes, and dislikes

_____ Explain why you like or dislike something

_____ Write about yourself (for example, information about your school) using simple language

A Read to Write

You're helping choose the majors for a new university that will open in a few years. Read through the list of recommended majors and the notes on each one. For the majors that have no notes (computer science and English), write your own. Then write in other majors that you would like to consider including in your program.

Name of Major	Notes	Include
Philosophy	Philosophy continues to bring in students at the best colleges.	☐
Finance	Graduates who succeed in finance often give a lot of money to the university, and they can make our school look better.	☐
Computer Science		☐
Psychology	In surveys, many students said they selected this major because it is "interesting."	☐
Dance	We need very talented students to make this a successful department. Scholarship money is available to help students afford our program.	☐
History	History is not a very popular major nowadays, but many students study it as a minor, or as an elective while studying other majors.	☐
English		☐
Agriculture	Fewer students are studying this recently, but the opportunities for graduates are getting better every year. With good promotion, we can make a successful department.	☐
Additional Majors You Want to Consider		
		☐
		☐
		☐

B Listen to Write

Listen to a short lecture with advice about majors that universities should offer. Take notes on a separate piece of paper. Use the advice and your notes to help you think about the majors on the list above, and add more majors to your list if possible. 🔊 Track 28

C Now Speak

Work with a partner. Compare your preferences. Discuss your reasons and try to persuade your partner to agree. Continue until you can agree on a final list, including 4 to 6 selected majors.

When you are done, discuss these questions:

1. Was it easy to agree with your partner on your list of majors? If not, how did one partner persuade the other?
2. In general, are you good at arguing and persuading people? Do you enjoy it? Why or why not?
3. Is it harder for you to argue in English? If not, why not? If so, how can you improve?

Lesson 1   Looking for a School

A   Authentic Text: A university brochure

Read the brochure. Then read the sentences and write *T* for true or *F* for false.

A Small-Town University with Big-City Conveniences

You can have it all! A high-quality university in a small town with all the conveniences of a major urban center. A safe and welcoming environment for students from around the world.

- You are never far away from shopping, healthcare and entertainment: only a five-minute walk from campus to downtown
- Only a short bus or train trip to the nearby city and easy access to an international airport
- Campus is located beside a very large nature park perfect for outdoor sports in all seasons
- Not far away (only 30 km) from the Kleisan Department for Research
- 50 km east of Magren Mountain for skiers and snowboarders

University residences are next to the school gym and library.

- Choose from 1-, 2-, or 4-bedroom apartments or single dormitory rooms.
- Meal plan for three campus restaurants.

Why should you be here?

- We are 50 km to the north of a city that offers jobs in technology for students and graduates.
- We rank in the top 10 for student satisfaction and number of students who find full-time jobs in less than six months after graduation.
- You can easily transfer credits from other colleges and universities.
- We have a reputation for high-quality education.

You won't find that anywhere else! Enroll now and get into the program of your choice!

1. The university is in a big city.
   _____
2. It is near downtown.
   _____
3. There's a nature park on campus.
   _____
4. It is close to a mountain.
   _____
5. Campus residences are close to the gym.
   _____
6. The university is 50 km east of an area with jobs in technology.
   _____

B   Vocabulary

Match the word or phrase on the left to the correct definition on the right.

1. environment •
2. conveniences •
3. enroll •
4. healthcare •
5. access •
6. satisfaction •
7. downtown •
8. credit •
9. transfer •
10. get into •

- a. the center of a city
- b. permission to use something
- c. a happy feeling; a feeling that something is right or good
- d. things that make life easier
- e. all the things that are around a person
- f. a unit of study as part of a degree or course
- g. to register as a student at a school
- h. medical help
- i. to be accepted into a program
- j. to move from one place to another

C   In Your World

Label the compass with directions: north, south, east, and west. Then talk with a partner:

What is around your school campus?

What is north, south, east, and west of you?

a _____

d _____      b _____

c _____

Adverbs of place

adverbs of place
Like many prepositions, an adverb of place tells us where an action happens or its location. Adverbs of place are different from prepositions because they do not have to be followed by nouns. They usually come after the main verb or its object.

I looked **around**, but I couldn't find my books.	I searched **everywhere**.
I have to go **back** to tell my teacher.	They built a school **nearby**.
The teacher always welcomes us **inside**.	We will look **outside**.

E Grammar Practice

Read the sentences and circle the correct answers.

1. I like this apartment because there's a park (nearby / outside).

2. We had some free time, so we walked (around / everywhere).

3. Let's sit (outside / next to) for lunch today.

4. Teresa is going shopping, but she'll come (inside / back) in time for dinner.

5. Why don't we sit (here / out), next to the window?

6. Please close the window before you go (out / across from).

7. Downtown is so crowded. There are people (everywhere / in)!

8. Please put your things right (under / there).

9. To get to campus, walk two blocks (north / around).

F Use the Language

Describing a campus

A.

B.

C.

D.

Work with a partner. Do not tell your partner which picture you chose. Describe the campus. Your partner will guess which picture you are describing. After he or she does, discuss why you chose that picture.

A Model Conversation

Read the conversation. Then listen. 🔊 Track 29

Leo: Hi, Martina. How are your classes?

Martina: I'm really not happy here. I'm thinking of changing schools.

Leo: That's a big decision. Why aren't you happy?

Martina: They offer limited programs here—mostly law or fine arts. I'm just not interested. It's so hard to stay motivated, and I don't want to fail. I want to study physical therapy.

Leo: Well, you'd better do some research on other schools.

Martina: It's so intense—I get stressed out. I don't know where to start!

Leo: That's okay. I can help you. Let's have a look at some websites together.

Martina: Thanks so much, Leo. You are such a good friend. But right now you'd better get to class. You've already had a few warnings about being late, right? Let's meet in the library after lunch.

Leo: I'll see you then.

> **Brief note**
> To "have a look" means to read or see something.

B Vocabulary

Study the words and phrases. Then practice saying them with a partner.

statistics

TESOL

environmental science

physical therapy

Match the words with the correct definitions.

1. warning •   • **a.** not much; not many

2. fail   •   • **b.** to not be successful at something; to not finish a class because of low grades

3. intense •   • **c.** advice to be careful about something

4. limited •   • **d.** stressful

Listen to the words again. Underline the stressed syllable in each word. Then practice saying the words out loud. 🔊 Track 30

statistics TESOL environmental science physical therapy warning fail intense limited

C In Your World

Discuss these questions with a partner.

• Why did you choose your program of study?

• Imagine you have to change schools. Where would you like to go? Why?

Brief note

In *had better*, the short form of *had* is usually used: *You had better* → *You'd better*. In informal conversation, people sometimes leave out *had*: *You better...*

D Grammar

had better (*not*) and *let's*

had better (*not*) + verb for suggestions and warnings	
Use *had better* to talk about things that someone should do. This is a strong way of making a suggestion. It has the meaning that there might be a negative result if the person does not do the action.	
+	The teacher is getting angry. You **had better stop talking** so much in class. He might fail that class. He**'d better get** a tutor.
-	This is a dangerous road. **You'd better not drive** so fast. He has an early class tomorrow. **He'd better not stay out** late tonight.
let's + verb for suggestions and proposals	
Use *let's* to make suggestions or proposals to someone. It is a contraction of "let us". **Let's meet** in the library after lunch. **Let's have a look** at some websites.	

Brief note

You can use *had better* in a question form: *Hadn't we better warn him about the test?* But it's more common to use *should* in questions.

E Grammar Practice

Write sentences using the given verbs and words or phrases from part D.

1. Classes start tomorrow, so we _____ (go) to bed early.

2. Your mother called and left a message. You _____ (call) her back.

3. You and I have a lot of work to do. _____ (meet) at the library this evening.

4. My sister might fail French. She _____ (hire) a tutor.

5. _____ (not work) on our project tonight. We can do it this weekend.

6. I want to sleep well tonight, so I _____ (not drink) any more coffee.

7. Professor Samuel can probably help us. _____ (talk) to her after class.

8. You _____ (do) some research before deciding to change schools.

F Use the Language

Getting advice

Read each student's situation. Work with a partner. Choose to be one of the students, and explain your problems. Your partner will ask questions to get more information and will give you advice and suggestions.

Brad: My father wanted me to study engineering so I can get a good job. That's why I applied to this school. But I really don't understand my courses, so I'm not doing well. I'm worried about failing. I don't want to study here. I guess I should talk to my parents about it, but I'm afraid to.

Cynthia: I'm in my first semester, and I'm lonely here. All my friends went to the local college in our town, but I came to this big school. I only go home about once a month, so I miss my friends. People here aren't friendly. I spend all my time by myself in the dorm. I like the classes, and my grades are good, but I want to make some friends.

Ramon: My university courses may not help me reach my goals. I should be working on my business—I buy and sell software. My business makes money, and I want to spend more time making it grow. Will a degree in programming help me run my business better? I'm not sure.

A Authentic Text: A university's homepage

Read the website.

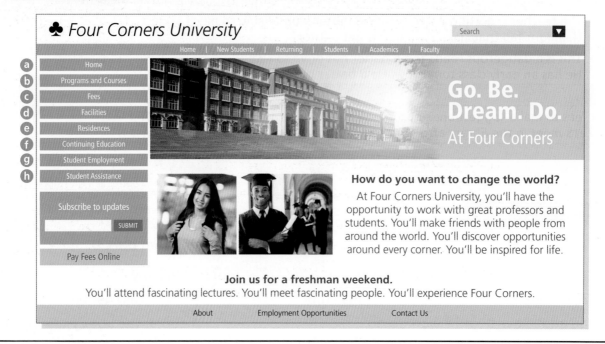

B Vocabulary

Fill in the blanks with the correct words and phrases from the box. Change the form if necessary.

inspire	life sciences	humanities	experience
faculty	assistance	discover	continuing education

1. Literature and languages are part of the _____ department.
2. If you are older and want to study part-time, contact someone in _____ _____.
3. Biology, chemistry, and environmental studies are in the _____ _____ department.
4. I couldn't decide on a major at first, but then I _____ a passion for art history.
5. Many people travel abroad in order to _____ new things.
6. Professors are members of the _____.
7. When choosing a major, it's good to think about what _____ you.
8. Students can contact an advisor for _____.

C Comprehension

Look at part A and write the correct letters. What should you click if you...

1. are a student with a problem? _____
2. want to know how much the school costs? _____
3. are looking for a job while you study? _____
4. want to ask a question about a major? _____
5. are an older adult and want to take a class? _____
6. want to stay in a dorm on campus? _____

Grammar

First conditional; *have* + object + *to* verb

first conditional	
A first conditional is an *if* sentence that expresses something that will be true in the future. It has an *if* clause in the simple present tense and result clause in the future tense.	
if clause (simple present) + result (*will* + verb)	If it **rains** tonight, she **will stay** home. If I **transfer** to another university, I**'ll be** happier.
result (*will* + verb) + *if* clause (simple present)	She **will stay** home **if** it **rains** tonight. I**'ll be** happier **if** I **transfer** to another university.
have + object + *to* verb	
Remember that you use *have* + object + *to* verb to give details about things that the subject has. These can be physical objects or not. For example: *I **have a chance to participate** in a school tour.*	

Grammar Practice

Brief note

Use a comma to separate two clauses when the sentence begins with *if*.

Match the two columns to make sentences.

1. If there isn't a pool on campus, •
2. I have too many books •
3. I'll transfer to another school •
4. If you want to get good grades, •
5. You'll get sick •
6. She has an opportunity •
7. If he doesn't get a scholarship, •

• a. if you don't get some rest.
• b. you will need to study harder.
• c. I'll have to go swimming at the one downtown.
• d. he'll have to work and save money for school.
• e. if I can't find classes I like here.
• f. to transfer to another school.
• g. to read this semester.

Use the Language

What's important to you?

What are the five most important factors to consider when you choose a school or university? Make a list.

1. _____
2. _____
3. _____
4. _____
5. _____

Compare your list with a partner's and give reasons for your answers. Are your lists similar or very different? Try to decide together on the most important factor for students to consider.

Then discuss these questions:

1. How did you learn about your school?

2. What factors did you research before you decided to attend your school?

Brief note

"A bunch of" means many.

A Model Conversation

Read the conversation. Then listen. 🔊 Track 31

Layla: Hi, Cecile. How's it going? Did you decide on a new school?

Cecile: No, not yet. I browsed a bunch of websites, but I'm still not sure what to do. Maybe it's not a good idea to transfer to a new school. What do you think I should do?

Layla: How about visiting some campuses? Then you can see the schools for yourself. Maybe you can sit in on some classes, too, if you want to.

Cecile: That's a great idea. I can't wait to explore some of the facilities, too. How about coming with me?

Layla: That sounds like fun. Let's make a list of three or four schools to visit and start planning.

Brief note

Use "How about" and *What about* to make suggestions. The structure is *How about/What about + V-ing*. For example: *How about visiting some campuses?*

B Vocabulary

1. You're planning to see a university campus. Put a check mark next to things you should do before you go.

   ____ **make an inquiry** with the admissions office

   ____ **find out** about transportation to the campus

   ____ **browse** the school website

   ____ **wander** around the campus

   ____ explore the **surrounding community**

   ____ **sit in on** classes

   ____ meet with a campus **recruiter**

   ____ **visit** the student center

2. In your opinion, what are the three most important things to do when you visit a new campus?

C Vocabulary Comprehension

Use the correct forms of the words and phrases from part B to complete the sentences.

Last week, I called a university to _____ _____ _____ about applying. I spoke with a woman in the admissions office, and she suggested that I make an appointment to speak with a(n) _____. She said they could answer all my questions about the school and its programs.

I made an appointment for the next day. Before my appointment, I _____ the school's website and other sites for information about the _____ _____. I _____ _____ there is a hospital, a shopping mall, and a nature park nearby.

The school is about three hours from my house, so I had to get up early to go to the meeting. Afterwards, I _____ around and explored the facilities, including the gym and the library. I talked with some current students. But I didn't _____ _____ _____ any classes. Maybe I'll _____ again next week to do that.

Grammar

think + (that) clause

think + (that) clause
Use this structure to give opinions or to give facts that you are unsure about.

I **think (that)** you have to study harder.
My father **doesn't think (that) I need** to change schools.
What do you **think (that) I should** do?
I **think (that)** you'd better visit some campuses.

> **Brief note**
> Including or leaving out the word *that* does not change the meaning.

E **Grammar Practice**

Fill in the blanks with the correct forms of the words from the box.

wander	think	get	that	find out

1. He doesn't have a car. I _____ he walks to school.

2. My sister likes to study. I think _____ she'll go to a good university.

3. Tony thinks I should _____ more about the university before transferring.

4. I don't think she'll need to work if she _____ a scholarship next year.

5. I think we should _____ around campus and look at the facilities.

F **Use the Language**

Schools in my area

Go online and research two local colleges or two famous ones. Use the information you find to fill in the chart.

School 1: _____	School 2: _____
Location:	Location:
Size (number of students):	Size (number of students):
Common majors:	Common majors:
Facilities:	Facilities:
Surrounding community:	Surrounding community:

Discuss the schools with a partner. Talk about how to prepare to go to each of them. Which college or university interests you more? Why?

A   Model Conversation

Read the conversation. Then listen. 🔘 Track 32

Martin: I'm not happy with any of the schools I looked at. I think I'll just keep going to this one.

Yuka: Why not take a semester off? It'll give you some time to think about what you want to do.

Martin: I'd like to travel, but I'd probably better finish my studies.

Yuka: Why don't you combine those ideas? Go abroad to study for a semester. There are lots of good exchange programs. You could learn a new language and culture, and still finish your studies.

Martin: That's not a bad idea. But it means I have to continue researching and thinking about a budget.

Yuka: I'll talk to my cousin in London. He studied in Canada, so he might have some suggestions.

Martin: The Canadian embassy is near my place, too. Maybe I'll go in and ask some questions about visas and insurance and stuff.

> **Brief note**
>
> "...and stuff" is an informal way of saying et cetera (etc.).

B   Vocabulary

Fill in the blanks with the correct words from the box.

visa   culture   budget   take … off   insurance   embassy   exchange program   combine

1. Before visiting a new country, you should learn a little about its _____.

2. To study in a foreign country, you need a student _____.

3. Allie is applying to a(n) _____ _____ so that she can study in Argentina.

4. It's important to make a(n) _____ so that you don't spend too much money.

5. My professor is going to _____ a year _____ to write a book.

6. When you put things together, you _____ them.

7. Students at universities need health _____.

8. Some students register with their country's _____ when they study abroad.

C   In Your World

Discuss the questions with a partner.

Imagine you are going abroad to study. You can go to any country in the world. Where would you go? Why?

D   Quick Review

Look back at the brief notes in this module. What word or phrase means…

1. …"many"? _____ _____ _____

2. …"to read or see something"? _____ _____ _____

3. …"to reach the same point as"? _____ _____ _____

E Grammar

keep/continue + gerund; why not and why don't

Brief note

It's more common to use *keep* + gerund in conversation and *continue* + gerund in writing or formal speaking.

keep/continue + gerund		why don't + subject + verb...?	why not + verb...?
Use this structure to talk about an action that you continue to do, often to reach a specific goal.		Use these phrases to make suggestions.	
If you want to get good grades, you have to **keep working** hard.	If you want to get good grades, you have to **continue working** hard.	**Why don't you combine** those ideas? **Why doesn't she transfer** her credits?	**Why not combine** those ideas? **Why not transfer** her credits?
I can't find a good job, but I'll **keep looking**.	I can't find a good job, but I'll **continue looking**.		

Brief note

You can also use *continue* with an infinitive: *If you continue to study hard, your grades will get better.*

F Grammar Practice

Underline the errors and rewrite the sentences correctly.

1. Dana wants to continue volunteer at the clinic to get experience for medical school.

   _____ .

2. Keep to researching English schools overseas.

   _____ .

3. Why don't you going to Montreal? You can keep learn English and French there.

   _____ .

4. I make a budget every month, but I keep to spend too much money.

   _____ .

5. Most schools continue to offering scholarships to students if they keep their grades high.

   _____ .

G Use the Language

Which university is best?

Read about the universities. Choose the one you think is best. On a separate piece of paper, write your reasons.

A.

B.

C.

A.
- Reasonable tuition and fees
- Opportunities to work on campus
- Many programs and courses
- Exciting student life
- Small, friendly town

B.
- Expensive tuition, but excellent reputation
- Well-known for business and international studies
- Opportunities to become an intern at a big company

C.
- Free tuition, but hard to get in
- Few programs and courses, but great reputation
- Excellent art and theater programs
- Near a big city

Find a partner. Discuss your opinions. Then rank the schools from 1 to 3.

Active Review

A Janet's Old Apartment

Listen to the news report and fill in the blanks. Then answer the questions. `Track 33`

The US Department of _____ has new research. It says that only 60 percent of students seeking an undergraduate degree at an American college or university finish their study program in six years.

The report looks only at full-time students _____ a four-year college or university for the first time in 2008. According to the researchers, 60 percent of these students completed their _____ program by 2014.

Why do many students keep _____ to graduate? It might be because they have _____ chances to change their majors. Some schools allow students to change or _____ their majors, while others don't allow this. Some researchers think that if changing majors becomes easier, more students will graduate. In other words, if students can find _____ with their subject, they will _____ studying. Also, some students change schools during their studies. If their new school doesn't let them _____ _____ from their old school, they will take longer to graduate and may not finish.

1. What did the researchers find out?

   _____.

2. List two reasons why students might fail to graduate.

   _____

   _____.

B Speaking

Work with a partner, doing research online if necessary. Discuss the questions.

1. How long do people usually stay at college or university in your country?
2. What other options are there for students in your country?
3. What are some other reasons why a college student might not graduate?

C Reminder

Some Module 3 Goals in Unit 6

Put a check mark (✓) next to the things you can do.

_____ Understand short, simple texts containing familiar vocabulary, including international words

_____ Describe past activities, events, and personal experiences

_____ Describe plans and alternatives

Warm Up: Brainstorming

Imagine you are a college or university recruiter. Prepare some interesting information about your university to share with students. (This can include real information about your school and/or your own ideas.)

B **School Information Fair**

Work with a partner to role-play a conversation at a school information fair. One of you will be a recruiter, and the other will be a student. Decide on your roles and read the descriptions carefully. Then role-play the conversation.

A. Recruiter

You are trying to interest good students in attending your school. Decide what type of school you work for. What information will you give the student, and what questions will you ask to find out if he or she is a good match for your school? Try to persuade the student to choose your school.

B. Possible Student

You are at an information fair trying to decide what college or university to attend. Decide on the type of school you are looking for. What questions will you ask the recruiter to help you decide if the school is right for you?

C **Write about it.**

Think about your role-play. Write a short email to your partner about your conversation.

- If you were the recruiter, invite the student to visit the campus and explain what he or she should do there.
- If you were the student, thank the recruiter for his or her time. Tell the recruiter if you are interested in the university or not, and give reasons.

_____

_____

_____

_____

_____

Module ③ Review

A Vocabulary

Remember and write...

1. ...four university majors.

   _____ _____ _____ _____

2. ...four directions on a compass.

   _____ _____ _____ _____

3. ...four adverbs of place.

   _____ _____ _____ _____

4. ...three comparative or superlative adverbs.

   _____ _____ _____

5. ...five adjectives you learned recently.

   _____ _____ _____ _____ _____

6. ...five verbs you learned recently.

   _____ _____ _____ _____ _____

B Grammar

Look back at the module. Circle the correct answers.

1. Class starts in ten minutes. We (are / have / had) better hurry.

2. Ryan keeps (arrive / arriving / to arrive) late to work.

3. If you (apply / applied / will apply) to that college, you'll get in.

4. Let's (look / to look / looking) into available apartments in this area.

5. Zoey is taking a semester off in order (travel / traveling / to travel) this fall.

6. Would you like (other / more / another) bowl of soup?

7. I dance fairly well, but my sister dances (more well / better / best) than me.

8. (Are / Would / Do) you rather have Chinese or Italian food for dinner?

9. (Why not / Why don't / What about) visit the campus this weekend?

10. Should I continue (study / studied / studying) here, or should I transfer?

11. I think (how / that / if) there are great opportunities in the medical field.

12. How about (spend / to spend / spending) the evening downtown?

13. Ian is very good at (persuade / persuading / to persuade) people.

14. What (other / another / else) should we ask the recruiter?

15. I left my phone at home, so I had to go (around / back / here) and get it.

C Pros and Cons

Work with a partner. Think about the pros and cons of studying abroad. Complete the chart below. Try to write at least three things in each box. Compare your chart with that of another pair.

Pros of studying abroad	Cons of studying abroad

D Some Advice

What advice do you have for a student who is trying to decide on a school and major? Discuss your advice with a partner.

Now write your name in the blank below. Read the letter. Then write a response on a separate piece of paper.

Dear _____,

I need some advice. At the moment, I'm studying interior design, but there's too much reading and not enough designing. I'd rather do creative things instead of just reading about them. I'm thinking about changing majors. But if I change my major now, I'll have to start another program from the beginning. I don't want to waste time.

Another option might be to keep the same major but change schools. But I don't want to change schools. I like this one. It's a prestigious school with an amazing faculty. The campus is beautiful, the facilities are great, and the surrounding area has so many conveniences. But I don't like studying interior design here. Do you think I should consider another school?

Let me know what you think.

Andy

E Debate

Before you debate, you think about a topic and decide your opinion. When you debate, you argue and try to persuade people to agree with you.

Read the statements below and decide on your opinion. Then form a small group and debate one of the statements. One person speaks at a time. When that person is finished, another person has an opportunity to speak. Continue until everyone talks. Can you persuade your group members to agree with you?

1. If you get a college degree, you will have a better life.
2. Going to a university near your home is better than going to a university in another city.
3. The government should help students pay their tuition.

A Break from School

Module 4 Goals

Talk about plans for your next holiday
Check written sentences for mistakes (for example, subject-verb agreement or article agreement)
Correctly use simple phrases you have learned for specific situations
Understand short, simple texts on familiar subjects
Summarize simple stories you have read, relying on the language used in the story
Understand simple texts, emails, and letters
Identify changes in the general topic of a discussion that is conducted slowly and clearly
Ask for and give opinions; agree and disagree

Preview

Look at pages 92 to 117. What pages are these things on?

screen names of chatters _____

a web browser _____

palm trees _____

two people eating and talking _____

Discuss

Talk about the questions with a partner.

1. Where do you think the photo was taken?

2. Is it a good idea for students to take a break from studying sometimes? Why or why not?

3. Do students from your country often study abroad? Where do they go?

4. Where would you like to study abroad? Why?

5. Do you chat with friends online? When, and about what?

Write

Choose one of the questions from above. Write a couple of sentences to answer it.

_____

_____

_____

Unit 7

Unit 8

Scan the QR code to watch a preview video.

★ Unit 7 · Time Off ★

Lesson 1 — Taking a Semester Off

A Model Conversation

Read the conversation. Then listen. 🔊 Track 34

Anna: Have you decided on a college to transfer to yet?

Mike: No, I haven't. I've read a lot of brochures, college websites, and blogs, but I still haven't found a program I like.

Anna: Well, have you considered taking a semester off? You know, to think about what program is right for you?

Mike: No, I've never thought about that. What could I do if I took time off?

Anna: Why not do some volunteer work or go traveling? My cousin volunteered at a center for the homeless last year, and one of my friends went backpacking in Thailand.

Mike: Thailand? I've never been to Asia. Hmm. Maybe. But if I take time off, I'll waste a whole semester. My parents might not like that.

Anna: Then you could stay in town and look for a job. You could earn some money and figure out your plans at the same time.

Mike: That's a possibility, too. I guess every option has pros and cons. I'll need to think about it some more.

> **Brief note**
> "Backpack" can be a noun or a verb. The gerund form of the verb is often used with *go*: *go backpacking*.

> **Brief note**
> "Pros" means good points, and "cons" means bad points.

B Vocabulary

Match the words and phrases from the box to the correct definitions.

a. whole	b. pros and cons	c. waste	d. possibility
e. earn	f. homeless	g. figure out	h. blog

1. _____ to get (something) in exchange for doing something
2. _____ people who do not have a place to live
3. _____ the good points and bad points of something
4. _____ complete; all of (something)
5. _____ to understand something or solve a problem by thinking
6. _____ something that might be done or might happen; an option
7. _____ a personal website about someone's opinions, experiences, etc.
8. _____ to use too much of something or not use it in a useful way

C In Your World

Imagine that a friend of yours is considering taking time off from school or work. You want to give your friend some advice. Make a list of pros and cons below. Then discuss your list with a partner.

Pros	Cons

Considering your list, what advice would you give your friend?

Present perfect; *still*, *never*, and *yet*

Yet is used in negative statements and questions in the present perfect.

present perfect	
The present perfect is often used to talk about experiences: things that happened (or didn't happen) at an unspecific time in the past. To form the present perfect, use *have/has* + past participle. For regular verbs, the past participle is the same as the simple past form: *have talked*, etc. The past participles of irregular verbs must be memorized.	
statements	I **have read** / I**'ve read** a lot of blogs.
negative statements	I **have not** / **haven't** cooked dinner yet.
questions and short answers	**Have** you **considered** taking a semester off? Yes, I **have**. / No, I **haven't**.

adverbs used with the present perfect			
adverb	**meaning**	**place in sentence**	**example**
still	until now	before have/has	I **still** haven't found a program I like.
never	not once	after have/has	I've **never** been to Asia.
yet	at any time before now	end of sentence	Have you decided on a school **yet**?

common irregular past participles					
be – been	begin – begun	buy – bought	choose – chosen	do – done	eat – eaten
fall – fallen	find – found	go – gone	hear – heard	leave – left	read – read
run – run	say – said	see – seen	sell – sold	sleep – slept	think – thought

---

E   Grammar Practice

Read the conversation and circle the correct answers.

1. **Woman:** I have (never / yet) been away from home. Any advice for going to college?

2. **Man:**   You'll need a place to live. Have you found an apartment (yet / never)?

3. **Woman:** That's true. No, I (have / haven't).

4. **Man:**   Why not look on the Internet? There are a lot of sites for student apartments. And (have / has) you bought books for your classes?

5. **Woman:** Yes, I (have / haven't).

6. **Man:**   Good. Have you (talking / talked) to your counselor about possible majors?

7. **Woman:** No, I haven't thought about that (still / yet).

F   Use the Language

Things I've done

Make a list of five interesting things you've done. Then list five things you've never done but want to do someday.

I've...	I've never..., but I want to someday

Discuss your lists with a partner. Give details about things you've done. Then talk about what you want to do, when do you want to do, and why.

A Authentic Text: An email

Read the text. Then answer the questions.

Hi, Mom and Dad.

I hope everyone is well back home. Not much is new here. I've become more and more unhappy with my classes and my grades. I need a change. I've spoken to a few people at the university about what to do.

I had a chat with my tutor last week. She says I should take time off and maybe take a few study skills courses to help me in the future. I spoke to some older students, too. None of them think taking a break is a bad idea. They said I should go traveling and think about things. But my roommate Jamie said I should stay put because things might get better. My advisor also suggested it was a bad idea to leave after only one semester. "It takes time to adjust to college," he said. So I still haven't been able to make up my mind. This whole situation is really getting on my nerves!

In my opinion, taking a break seems to be a good idea, but I'm still uncertain. I'll call you this weekend to discuss it and get a few ideas from you.

Lucy

Send   A   📎   🖼   🔗   ☺   🗑 | ▼

> **Brief note**
> You can use "more and more + adjective" to describe a feeling or quality that gets stronger over time.

---

1. Who has Lucy spoken to?   **2.** What did she ask them?

B Comprehension

Read the statements. Circle true or false.

1. Lucy's tutor believes she should take some study skills courses.	true	false
2. The older students think taking time off to travel is a bad idea.	true	false
3. Her roommate believes she should continue studying.	true	false
4. Lucy thinks a break isn't a good idea.	true	false

C Vocabulary

Match the words and phrases to the correct definitions.

1. advisor   •   • **a.** to annoy a lot
2. uncertain   •   • **b.** to become more comfortable in a new situation
3. make up one's mind •   • **c.** a counselor; a person who gives advice
4. stay put   •   • **d.** not sure
5. adjust (to)   •   • **e.** to decide on something
6. get on one's nerves •   • **f.** to stay where you are (informal)

D Vocabulary: More irregular past participles

Fill in the blanks with the correct past participle from the box.

| speak – spoken   get – gotten   take – taken   become – become   make – made   give – given |

1. He's my favorite teacher because he's never _____ us any homework!

2. Rosa has graduated from medical school and _____ a doctor.

3. I've _____ some good courses on US history.

4. Have you _____ with your parents about leaving school yet?

5. For our film studies class, we've _____ a short movie about dogs.

6. Michael's grades arrived in the mail yesterday, but I still haven't _____ mine.

E Grammar

Simple past vs. present perfect; *few* vs. *a few*; *none* (of)

past simple	present perfect
Use the simple past to talk about actions finished at specific times in the past. Use the present perfect to talk about actions that aren't finished or that happened in the past when the specific time is unknown or unimportant.	
I **had** a chat with my tutor last week. I **saw** a student adviser on Monday.	I've **done** a lot of research. I've **spoken** to a few people at the university.

few vs. *a few*		*none of* + pronoun or (determiner +) noun	
Few and *a few* come before plural nouns. *Few* means "not many" (negative), and *a few* means "some" (positive).		The pronoun *none* can be followed by *of* and then a pronoun or a singular or plural noun. Use a singular verb if the noun or pronoun is singular, and a plural verb if it is plural.	
I'd like to help you, but I have **few** ideas.	Maybe I can help you! I have **a few** ideas.	**None of the food / None of it** is good.	**None of the people / None of them** are eating.

F Grammar Practice

Circle the correct answers.

1. Have you (spoke / spoken) to your advisor about your schedule yet?
2. My sister still (didn't visit / hasn't visited) me at school.
3. We (have taken / took) two exams this month.
4. (Did they see / Have they seen) a movie last night?
5. Nick (was never / has never been) to Australia, but he'd like to go.
6. I've adjusted to living on campus well. I've had (few / a few) problems.
7. They canceled the class because (few / a few) students wanted to take it.
8. Will you drop by my office, please? I have (few / a few) things to discuss with you.
9. (None of / A few of) the students were late. Everybody was here on time.
10. None of the pizza (was / were) left—you ate it all!
11. None of the students (is / are) listening to the lecture.

G Use the Language

Giving advice

1. Here or on a separate piece of paper, write a short note to a partner about a problem you've had at school. Explain the problem, name at least two people you've spoken to about it, and summarize their advice.

2. Exchange notes with your partner.
   - Check your partner's note for any mistakes.
   - Read the note and decide which advice is the best. If neither is good, come up with your own advice.
   - Write a reply to your partner, giving your opinion...

3. Read the reply to your note. Do you agree with your partner's advice? Why or why not?

Lesson 3 Going Home

A Model Conversation

Read the conversation. Then listen. Has Tommy made any decisions? Track 35

Tommy: It's beautiful outside today, isn't it?
Fiona: Yeah! And it's nice to see you in such a good mood.
Tommy: I really am. I've finished my final exams, and soon I'm going home for six months.
Fiona: Oh, I forgot—you're taking a semester off, right? You mentioned that a while ago.
Tommy: Yeah, I haven't been to my hometown in almost a year. I'm dying to see everyone, especially my little brother. He's eight.
Fiona: That's great. But what are you going to do for six months?
Tommy: I'll be busy. I'm going to teach my brother to play baseball, and I'll work at my parents' restaurant.
Fiona: Will you have any time to relax and be lazy?
Tommy: Sure. I haven't seen my high school friends since we graduated, so it'll be great to catch up with them, too. We'll spend lots of time at the beach.
Fiona: Sounds like a good plan.

B Vocabulary

Listen to the words. Repeat. Then write the words next to the correct definitions.
Track 36

| busy | dying (to) | almost | especially | catch up (with) | mention | beach | lazy |

Definition	Word(s)
1. wanting or looking forward to doing something very much (informal)	
2. more than usual or more than others	
3. an area of land next to the sea or a lake	
4. to talk to someone you have not seen for a long time	
5. having many things to do; active	
6. not wanting to work hard or be active	
7. a little less than; nearly	
8. to bring (something) up; to talk about, usually briefly	

C Vocabulary Comprehension

Fill in the blanks with the correct words and phrases from part B.

1. Linda loves all kinds of exercise, _____ hiking.
2. Your family sounds so interesting. I'm _____ to meet them.
3. If you're not _____ on Saturday, let's go to the beach.
4. My roommate is really _____! He never cleans or does the dishes.
5. Kim's cell phone is old—she's had it for _____ five years.
6. An old friend of mine is in town, so we're meeting for dinner to _____ _____.

D About You

Imagine that you are taking a break from school and spending it in your hometown. What are some things that you would like to do during this time? Think of three things that you would like to do and share your answers with a partner.

E Grammar

Time expressions with the present perfect; empty *it*

time expressions with the present perfect	
You can use *since*, *for*, and *in* with the present perfect to talk about how long ago something began.	
since + event / point in time	*since* + clause
I haven't seen my friends **since graduation**. We've lived here **since January**.	I haven't seen my friends **since we graduated**. He's been my best friend **since I was 5**.
present perfect + *for* + period of time	present perfect + *in* + period of time
I haven't been to my hometown **for almost a year**. She's thought about it **for several weeks**.	I haven't been to my hometown **in almost a year**. He hasn't bought new clothes **in a long time**.

empty *it*			
Some sentences have an empty *it* subject. It is "empty" because it doesn't replace a noun.			
weather	It's sunny today. It'll rain tomorrow.	time	It's 4:15. It's almost noon.
day/date	It's Friday. It's April 10.	distance	It's 200 km to my hometown.
adj. + infinitive	It's nice to meet you. (=To meet you is nice.) **It** will be great to see them.		

F Grammar Practice

Put the words in order to make sentences.

1. have / six / played / the piano / months / I / for

   _____.

2. three / English / studied / for / I / years / have

   _____.

3. in / I / weeks / haven't / two / TV / watched

   _____.

4. him / known / I've / was / since / young / I

   _____.

5. 2016 / worked / since / he / library / in / the / has

   _____.

G Use the Language

It's been…

Complete the sentences with information that is true for you.

> I haven't eaten ice cream _____.
>
> I haven't watched a great movie _____.
>
> I haven't been to a zoo _____.

Write two more sentences about things you have or haven't done and how long it has been since you did them.

_____

_____

Discuss your sentences you wrote with another student. Are you sad you haven't done these things for a while? Why haven't you done them?

A　Authentic Text: An online chat

Read the chat. What kind of vacation does the woman want to take?

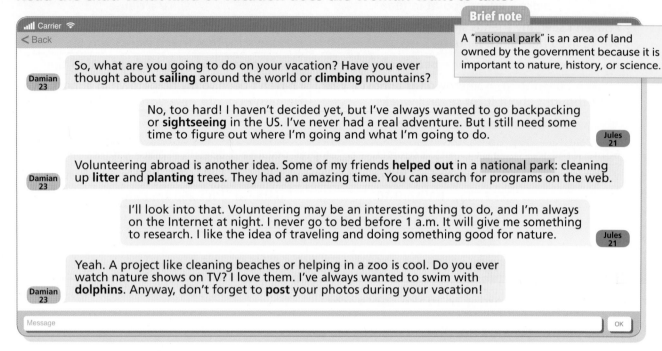

Brief note

A "national park" is an area of land owned by the government because it is important to nature, history, or science.

Damian 23: So, what are you going to do on your vacation? Have you ever thought about **sailing** around the world or **climbing** mountains?

Jules 21: No, too hard! I haven't decided yet, but I've always wanted to go backpacking or **sightseeing** in the US. I've never had a real adventure. But I still need some time to figure out where I'm going and what I'm going to do.

Damian 23: Volunteering abroad is another idea. Some of my friends **helped out** in a national park: cleaning up **litter** and **planting** trees. They had an amazing time. You can search for programs on the web.

Jules 21: I'll look into that. Volunteering may be an interesting thing to do, and I'm always on the Internet at night. I never go to bed before 1 a.m. It will give me something to research. I like the idea of traveling and doing something good for nature.

Damian 23: Yeah. A project like cleaning beaches or helping in a zoo is cool. Do you ever watch nature shows on TV? I love them. I've always wanted to swim with **dolphins**. Anyway, don't forget to **post** your photos during your vacation!

Message　[OK]

Read the messages again. Put a check mark next to the true sentences.

1. ☐ He likes watching TV shows about nature.
2. ☐ She is never on the Internet at night.
3. ☐ She's always wanted to take a boat trip.
4. ☐ His friends had a bad time while they were volunteering.
5. ☐ She's been on exciting trips before.
6. ☐ She's going to think while she is traveling.
7. ☐ They're both interested in doing something good for nature.
8. ☐ He wants to see pictures of her trip.

B　Vocabulary

Read the chat again. With a partner, match each bold word to its correct definition.

1. _____ visiting the famous places in a specific location
2. _____ volunteer one's help
3. _____ to put (a message, photo, etc.) on a website for others to see
4. _____ putting plants into the ground to grow

Write the correct bold word from the chat under each picture.

5. _____　6. _____　7. _____　8. _____

C　About You

What have you always wanted to do while traveling? Think about three activities—places to visit, food to eat, people to meet, etc. Tell other students about them. What do they think about your ideas?

D Grammar

ever, never, and always; while and during

Brief note

Use *ever* only in questions and negative statements.

simple present with *ever / never / always*	present perfect with *ever / never / always*
You can use *ever*, *never*, and *always* with the present perfect to talk about people's past experiences. We also use them with the simple present to talk about people's lives now.	
Do you **ever** watch nature shows on TV? I **never** go to bed before midnight. She is **always** on the Internet at night.	Have you **ever** thought about sailing? I've **never** had a real adventure. She has **always** wanted to travel.
during + noun	*while* + clause
Both *during* and *while* communicate that something is happening at the same time as another thing. The preposition *during* is followed by a noun, but the conjunction *while* is followed by a clause (subject + verb).	
What do you enjoy doing **during** your time off? Post your photos **during** your vacation!	I'll figure out what I want **while** I'm traveling. Please write to me **while** you're abroad.

Brief note

In the present perfect, *ever*, *never*, and *always* come before the past participle.

E Grammar Practice

Circle the correct words to complete the short conversations.

1. A: Do you (ever / never / while) eat lunch on campus?
   B: Yes, I do. I usually eat outside (during / always / while) I do my homework.

2. A: Have you (during / ever / while) had a job?
   B: Yes, I have. I worked in a bookstore (ever / while / during) the summer.

3. A: Have you (while / during / ever) been to New York?
   B: No, I've (always / ever / never) been there. But I'd love to go.

4. A: Do you ever fall asleep (while / during / never) you're in class?
   B: No, I've never fallen asleep (while / during / ever) a class.

5. A: I've (ever / never / always) gone sailing. Have you?
   B: Yes, once. My family rented a boat (while / during / ever) a trip to California.

6. A: What would you like to do (while / during / always) you're in Japan?
   B: I've (ever / always / never) wanted to climb Mt. Fuji.

F Use the Language

Find out about your classmates.

Do some research on your classmates. First, choose a topic. Then, on a separate piece of paper, write a questionnaire (a list of questions) to ask the other students in your class. The topic could be on places in town, unusual foods, visiting tourist sites, dangerous activities, or your own idea. Make all of the questions yes/no questions.

Find out three students' information. Then write a paragraph about each of the students you interviewed.

Lesson 5 — Part-time Job

A Model Conversation

Read the conversation. Then listen. Track 37

Brenda: Oh, A.C.—nice to see you! How long have you worked here?

A.C.: Since school finished. So, since December. I'm taking next semester off, so I wanted a temporary job.

Brenda: What's it like?

A.C.: Well, the hours and the wages aren't bad, and I like the work so far.

Brenda: You're a friendly guy, so I'm sure you're good at customer service. Have they made you the boss yet?

A.C.: Haha. No, but I get some good tips. And they've made me assistant manager.

Brenda: Congratulations! How long have you had that position?

A.C.: Three weeks. The manager doesn't know much about computers, so I think he chose me for my IT skills.

Brenda: So far, it sounds great. Are you going to quit when you go back to school?

A.C.: I might stay. The company provides chances for advancement. I'm learning about organization and leadership. Maybe I'll get a higher-level job with this company after graduation.

Brief note

"provide" something is to give it to someone or make it available.

Brief note

A "tip" is extra money that customers give when an employee does a good job of helping them.

B Vocabulary

List four items for each category below. Use words from part B, words from previous units, and your own ideas. Share your answers with a partner.

advancement   leadership   customer service   organization   IT skills   wages

Working Conditions	Work Skills

C About You

Below are some common jobs that college students do. Work with a partner. Write down other common jobs that students do.

pizza delivery person   babysitter   waiter   tutor   cashier

- _____ • _____ • _____ • _____ • _____
- _____ • _____ • _____ • _____ • _____

Which of these jobs have you had before? Which would like to do? Why? Discuss your answers with your partner.

D Grammar

How long questions with the present perfect; *so far*

Brief note

Look back at lesson 3 of this unit to review time expressions used in answers to these questions.

How long + present perfect questions
Use *how long* + present perfect to ask about the period of time something has lasted, from the beginning until now. The answer often uses *since* or *for*.
A: **How long** have you worked there?   B: **Since** school finished. / **For** three weeks.

so far
So far means "up until now." We use it when we expect an action to continue. It usually comes at the beginning or the end of a sentence.
I like the work **so far**. / **So far**, I like the work.   It sounds great **so far**. / **So far**, it sounds great.

E Grammar Practice

Brief note

Like *yet*, *so far* talks about the time before now, but *yet* is only used in negatives and questions; *so far* can be used in any kind of sentence.

Put the words in order to make sentences.

1. long / he / has / how / games / computer / played

   _____?

2. lived / you / long / have / how / there

   _____?

3. has / she / the / been / assistant manager / long / how

   _____?

4. I / so / my / love / far / new / job

   _____.

F Read to Write

Read the journal entry about a video game. Underline the uses of the present perfect.

> I got a new game last week. It's called *Monster Dungeon*. It's the coolest game I've ever played! The graphics are so real, and the fighting moves are extremely fast and natural. I don't know how much time I've spent playing so far, but I should reach level 50 tomorrow.
>
> My friend Kyle is coming over tomorrow to play with me. It'll be great to see him again. I haven't seen him for about three months. He's been away at school. I told him about the game, and he said he's never played a game like it. It'll be great to catch up with him.

G Use the Language

Write about one of the activities. Then share your answers with other students and ask them about theirs.

Option 1: Choose a TV program you watch a lot. Write a few sentences about what has happened on the show recently, or since it started. What do you like about it?

Option 2: Describe a book or comic you're reading these days. Write a few sentences about how long you've read it, what's happened so far, and why you like it.

Option 3: Choose a video game you play a lot. Write a few sentences about how long you've played it, what's happened so far (best level, score, etc.), and why you like it.

A Semester Off

Listen to the conversation and fill in the blanks with the words that you hear. 🔊 Track 38

Marni: Have you decided on your courses for next semester _____?

Billy: No, I haven't. I'm taking next semester off. I don't like my major, so I've been looking for another program. But _____ _____ I haven't found one I like. _____ of them are very interesting.

Marni: Really? You've never _____ this. _____ _____ have you felt this way?

Billy: _____ the semester started, so for almost four months. I've done some research on other _____.

Marni: Great. Have you _____ _____ your mind yet?

Billy: No, I'm still uncertain. I might get a part-time job. Or maybe I'll move back home _____ I think about my future.

Marni: Have you _____ thought about going traveling? My friend did that _____ _____. He loved it. He did some backpacking and _____, and helped clean up a beach.

Billy: No, I've _____ thought about that. Sounds really interesting. I'll research it _____ the semester break.

Check Your Options

Imagine that you are in Billy's situation. Research different travel opportunities for young people taking a year off from school. Make notes on the ones you like best.

	Billy's research notes:

Write and Talk

Work with a partner. On a separate piece of paper, write a conversation Billy and Marni might have after Billy has researched his options. Then role-play your conversation.

Reminder

Some Module 4 Goals in Unit 7

Put a check mark (✓) next to the things you can do.

_____ Talk about plans for your next holiday

_____ Correctly use simple phrases you have learned for specific situations

_____ Check written sentences for mistakes (for example, subject-verb agreement or article agreement)

A   Listen to Speak

Listen to an advisor asking a student some questions. Fill out the student's information on the form as you listen. ⊙ Track 39

Student Information Questionnaire		
Name:		
Work: Yes ☐ No ☐	**Traveling:** Yes ☐ No ☐	
Details:	**Details:**	

B   Write to Speak

The advisor also has to ask questions about the topics below. Write questions that the advisor can ask to find out details about a student's interests and experiences.

- Living at home _____

- Studying abroad _____

- Volunteering _____

- Other activities: _____

Now prepare a form for those topics. It can be similar to the one above.

C   Now Speak

Role-play a conversation between an advisor and a student. Partner A is the advisor. Partner B is the student.

1. Partner A ask your questions from activity B and fill out your form. Partner B should use true information in his or her answers, if possible. Get more details by asking follow-up questions.

2. Partner A give your opinion about what you think partner B should do if he or she takes time off.

3. Switch roles and role-play again.

Lesson 1   Canada or the USA?

A   Model Conversation

Brief note

"Toronto" is a Canadian city in the province of Ontario, and "San Diego" is an American city in the state of California.

Read the conversation. Then listen. ⏵Track 40

Anika: What do you think about studying abroad, Albert?

Albert: I think it's a fun way to learn about new cultures, people, and food. Why?

Anika: Well, I'm seriously thinking about doing it. But I'm not sure whether I should go to Canada or the US. I can go to Toronto or San Diego. But both cities might be great. What's your opinion about Canada?

Albert: Well, I don't think you'll like the snow and the freezing temperatures, Anika. I'm sure you would rather be in San Diego, enjoying the sunny beaches and the nightlife.

Anika: You're right. I don't like the cold. But I'm also not a fan of hot and humid weather. Also, I'm not sure if I want to go for a year or a semester. A year seems like an extremely long time.

Albert: I don't agree. You need a year to really get to know a place. Have you decided if you want to live with a homestay family or in a dorm? Having a suitable place to live is the main thing you need to have a good time studying abroad.

Anika: Yeah, I agree. I haven't thought about it.

Albert: Well, in my opinion, staying with a family is great if you want to study, but a dorm is better for making friends. I think a dorm is much better. But you should research things thoroughly before you decide.

B   Vocabulary

Match the words and phrases to the correct definitions.

a. main	**b.** seriously	**c.** nightlife	**d.** be a fan of
e. freezing	**f.** extremely	**g.** suitable	**h.** thoroughly

1. the most important _____
2. activities and kinds of entertainment that happen at night _____
3. completely or perfectly _____
4. very; greatly _____
5. right for someone or something _____
6. very cold _____
7. involving a lot of thought; sincerely _____
8. an expression used to show that a person likes something very much _____

C   Comprehension

Listen and read the conversation again. Then answer the questions with a partner. What three decisions does Anika need to make? What are Anika's options? ⏵Track 40

Decision 1: _____ Options: _____ or _____

Decision 2: _____ Options: _____ or _____

Decision 3: _____ Options: _____ or _____

D   About You

Discuss these questions with a partner.

What advice would you give Anika on each of the above decisions? Why?

E Grammar

whether and if

whether (option 1 *or* option 2)	if (option 1 *or* option 2)
We can use *whether/if... or...* to talk about two options or possibilities.	
Do you know **whether** you will study abroad **or** not? I don't know **whether** I should go to Canada or the US.	I'm not sure **if** I want to go for a year **or** a semester. Have you decided **if** you want to live with a family **or** in a student dorm?

F Grammar Practice

Put the words in order to make sentences. Answers may vary.

1. Europe / I want to / I / America / if / or / can't decide / study in

   _____ .

2. whether / one semester / for / do you know / you will / or / a year / study

   _____ ?

3. I want to / the dorms / live in / I don't know / with a homestay / if / or

   _____ .

4. doesn't know / study in / he'll / Sam / whether / China / or / Japan

   _____ .

5. study abroad / next year / she'll / if / or not / hasn't decided / Maria

   _____ .

G Use the Language

Whether or not

1. Write a list of three decisions (real or made-up) you need to make. They can be about school, friends, going out, which university or subject to choose, or another subject. Each decision needs two options.

2. Work with other students. Tell them about the decisions you need to make. Listen to their opinions and let them know if you agree or not. Make sure everyone gives reasons for their opinions.

Decision	Option 1	Option 2

3. Did you get any help with your decisions? Tell the class about your decisions and your partners' opinions.

A　Authentic Text: A study-abroad web page

Read the web page about studying abroad in the US.

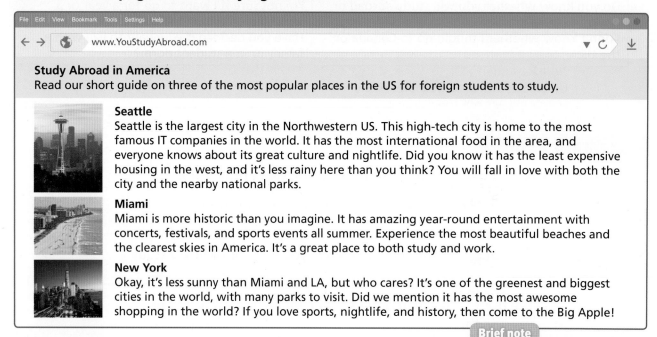

Study Abroad in America
Read our short guide on three of the most popular places in the US for foreign students to study.

Seattle
Seattle is the largest city in the Northwestern US. This high-tech city is home to the most famous IT companies in the world. It has the most international food in the area, and everyone knows about its great culture and nightlife. Did you know it has the least expensive housing in the west, and it's less rainy here than you think? You will fall in love with both the city and the nearby national parks.

Miami
Miami is more historic than you imagine. It has amazing year-round entertainment with concerts, festivals, and sports events all summer. Experience the most beautiful beaches and the clearest skies in America. It's a great place to both study and work.

New York
Okay, it's less sunny than Miami and LA, but who cares? It's one of the greenest and biggest cities in the world, with many parks to visit. Did we mention it has the most awesome shopping in the world? If you love sports, nightlife, and history, then come to the Big Apple!

> **Brief note**
> Check the Grammar Reference to learn more about using -er/-est comparatives and superlatives.

B　Vocabulary

Complete the description of a city using the words in the box.

high-tech	historic	fell in love	year-round	festivals	green

I want to study in the Big Apple because it is a very ❶ _____ city with many IT companies. At the same time, it is also a ❷ _____ city because of its famous older buildings such as the Empire State building and monuments such as the Statue of Liberty. Since I love nature, living in a ❸ _____ city is also important. There is a huge park called Central Park in Manhattan. There is also a very famous national park in the town of Stillwater, where you can see historic sites from the American Revolution. Although the ❹ _____ sports events and ❺ _____ in cities such as Miami are interesting, the nightlife in New York is much more exciting. Oh, did I mention the shopping? I love shopping! I visited New York last year on vacation, and I just ❻ _____ with the city.

> **Brief note**
> New York City is informally called the *Big Apple*.

C　In Your World

Read the web page again. Answer the questions.

1. Which city is …
   a. the biggest?
   b. the rainiest?
   c. the least expensive?
   d. the greenest?
   e. the clearest?

2. Which city has …
   a. the most awesome music and games?
   b. the most amazing shopping?
   c. national parks close to the city?
   d. a lot of historic places and beaches?
   e. the cheapest housing in the area?

3. Which city would you prefer to study in?

D Grammar

Comparative and superlative adjectives: *more/most, less/least*; *both* A *and* B

comparative adjectives (A *is less/more* + adjective *than* B)	superlative adjectives (A *is the least/most* + adjective)
Comparatives compare two things. Superlatives describe the greatest or lowest degree. *Less* is a comparative. It means the opposite of *more*. *The least* is a superlative. It means the opposite of *most*.	
Miami is **more historic** than you imagine. It's **less rainy** here than you think. It's **less sunny** than Miami or Los Angeles.	It has **the most international** food in the area. Did you know it has **the least expensive** housing in the West? That state has **the least cloudy** skies in America.

both A *and* B
When you use *both* A *and* B, remember that A and B must be the same type or part of speech (noun, verb, infinitive, etc.).
You will fall in love with **both** the city **and** the nearby national parks. It offers a great place **both** to study **and** to work.

E Grammar Practice

Underline the error in each sentence. Write the correction.

1. I like both Canada the USA. _____

2. I disagree. This country is least dangerous than America. _____

3. I think Rio is most beautiful city in the world. _____

4. In my opinion, Brazil is the more exciting country in South America. _____

5. My city more interesting than LA. _____

6. This city is more quiet New York. ◄──────────── _____

7. Vancouver is the last rainy city in Canada. _____

8. Washington is less expensiver than Dallas. _____

9. I think you'll enjoy both the nature or the history. _____

10. It is a great place both to relax and goes sightseeing. _____

> **Brief note**
> Although *more quiet...than* is correct, *quieter... than* is also acceptable. The usage of *quieter... than* is more common in American English.

F Use the Language

Rate your city

Complete the chart below. Score your city from 1 star (bad) to 4 stars (great). Then write some reasons. Discuss your scores with a group and agree on a group score.

Your city's rating	Reasons
☆☆☆☆	1.
	2.
	3.
	4.

Then compare your city to two other cities. These can be in your country or in another country. Decide which city is best and explain why. Tell the class about your decision. Do they agree with you?

A Authentic Text: A language school's web page

Read the web page about language schools.

 **New York College (NYC) vs. Springville Center (SC)**

We asked international students about the most important factors to consider when choosing a place to study English abroad. We compared two top English schools in Springville and New York. Here are the students' answers.

Entry Requirements
SC is as easy as NYC to get into. Both colleges need an intermediate level of English (TOEFL iBT scores of 80+).

Class Size
NYC has fewer students in each class (15) than SC (18), but NYC is the bigger college (NYC 400 / SC 175). SC feels less crowded than NYC when walking around the area.

Campus
SC campus has fewer buildings than NYC. Also, SC is a much older college, so the buildings are less modern than the high-tech ones on NYC's campus.

Accommodations
Students say NYC dorms are as comfortable and new as SC's, but fewer NYC students live on campus. That's because many live with homestay families who live 5 km and farther from the college.

Facilities
The facilities at NYC, such as the library, IT center, and classrooms, are as good as those at SC. But NYC campus has a new fitness center and some of the tastiest and most affordable restaurants nearby.

Location
SC offers a beautiful green campus 20 km away from the nearest city. That means it has less noise and traffic than NYC. It's a great place for quiet study, but NYC has better nightlife and cultural events.

Activities
SC has fewer evening events than NYC. However, SC has many different social clubs for students to meet and chat with other students. Both places scored high in our survey for sports activities and cultural events.

B Vocabulary

Fill in the blanks with the correct words and phrases from the box.

modern	entry requirement	affordable	traffic	cultural events	comfortable	survey

1. Students do not have a lot of money, so they often look for _____ places to eat.

2. One good thing about living in the city is the _____ technology.

3. The new classroom desks are wider and much more _____ than the tiny old ones.

4. I enjoy going to _____ because I like to learn about different cultures, countries, and people.

5. The _____ asks for students' opinions on their campus, classes, and teachers.

6. Passing this exam is a(n) _____ for this high school.

7. The _____ in New York is heavy. It can take a long time to travel by car.

C In Your World

Work with a partner. Discuss which campus you would prefer to study at. Which factors are most important to you?

Grammar

Comparing using *less*, *fewer,* and (*not*) *as... as...*

less + adjective / uncountable noun	*fewer* + countable noun
Less is used to compare adjectives and uncountable nouns. *Fewer* is used to compare countable nouns. Both words mean the opposite of more.	
SC feels **less** crowded than NYC. It has **less** noise and traffic than the city university.	NYC has **fewer** students in each class than SC. **Fewer** NYC students live on campus.
as + adjective + *as*	
You can use *as + adjective + as* to say two things are the same, or *not as + adjective + as* to describe their differences.	
NYC dorms are **as** comfortable and new **as** SC's dorms. (=The schools' dorms are equally comfortable.) SC is **not as** noisy **as** the city college. (=SC is less noisy than the city college.)	

> **Brief note**
>
> When you want to say one thing is less than another, you can either use *less than* or *not as* + adjective + *as*. *This show is less interesting than I thought.* *This show is not as interesting as I thought.*

Grammar Practice

Put the words in (parentheses) in the correct order and write the sentence.

1. This language school (as / is / as / big) the other language school.

   _____.

2. The classes here (as / those / as / small / are) at the National University.

   _____.

3. Our campus (fewer / places / has / green) than the other university.

   _____.

4. The (are / entry / difficult / requirements / less) at the Polytechnic University than here.

   _____.

5. I think the (modern / are / facilities / less) at the other university.

   _____.

Use the Language

The best place to study

Work with a partner. Think of an ideal university to attend. It does not have to be a real university. Fill in the table with information about your ideal university. When you are done, compare your university with another group's. Then decide which university is the best place to go.

Name of university:	Class size:	Facilities:
	Campus:	Location:
	Accommodations:	Activities:

A Model Conversation

Read the conversation. Then listen. 🎧 Track 41

Monica: Oh, wow! You can read the Spanish news on this website **free of charge**.

Lucas: Really? Great! We can use that for our group project.

Monica: Yeah. Hmm. You know, it's actually a really **convenient** website. With this, I think we could finish early and go to the student party tonight. I really want to go.

Lucas: So do I. But we have an exam tomorrow, remember?

Monica: I know, but I don't want to spend all night studying.

Lucas: Well, neither do I. But we have to do well in this class if we want to study in Spain next year. Why don't we study together? You can help me work on my **pronunciation**, and I can **quiz** you on the vocabulary.

Monica: Oh, all right. Where do you want to meet?

Lucas: The library has Wi-Fi, so we can **download** all the class notes and watch the lecture videos with **subtitles**. Want to meet there at 7:00?

Monica: Let's meet at 6:00 and **grab** dinner first.

Brief note
"Wi-Fi" is a place that offers wireless Internet access.

B Vocabulary

Look at the bold expressions used in the conversation. Match each word or phrase with the correct definition.

1. free of charge
2. convenient
3. pronunciation
4. grab
5. download
6. quiz
7. subtitles
8. skip

a. the words of a movie, TV show, etc. shown on the screen, often in a different language
b. easy to do or use without much trouble
c. to ask questions to check someone's knowledge
d. to copy or move files from one device to another
e. to not attend (an event); to miss
f. the way people make sounds to form words and sentences
g. at no cost
h. to get and eat quickly

C In Your World

Listen to the conversation again and circle true or false. 🎧 Track 41

1. The library has Wi-Fi.   true   false
2. They both have to take an exam.   true   false
3. Both students are going to the student party tonight.   true   false
4. They are both going to lunch.   true   false
5. The Spanish website will help with their exam.   true   false
6. Lucas thinks the website is really convenient.   true   false

Which of the following ways to study a foreign language do you think is the best? Rank the methods below from 1 (best) to 4 (worst).

_____ read the news   _____ watch a movie with subtitles

_____ use a computer for vocab and grammar exercises   _____ write a blog

Grammar

can and *could* for possibility; phrases for agreement

can/can't + base verb		*could* + base verb	
We use *can* and *could* to talk about things that are possible.			
You **can help** me with my pronunciation. I **can't go** to the party.		We **could finish** early and go to the party. We **could invite** our classmates.	
phrases for agreement			
You can use *so, too,* and *neither* to say that you agree with someone.			
agreeing with a positive sentence		**agreeing with a negative sentence**	
A: I want to go to the party.	B: **So** do I.	A: I don't want to study.	B: **Neither** do I.
A I'm hungry now.	B: **So** am I. (Me too.)	A: I'm not hungry yet.	B: **Neither** am I. (Me **neither**.)

Brief note

If you are agreeing with a statement that uses *have* or a modal verb, use the same verb in your response:
A: I have been to Canada. B: So have I.   *A: I can't swim. B: Neither can I.*

E **Grammar Practice**

Fill in the blanks with the correct words and phrases from the box. One word can be used more than once.

could film	neither	so do	can practice	too

1. A: We _____ together. I think it'll be fun!   B: _____ I. Excellent idea.
2. A: I think listening to English music is good practice.   B: Me _____. Especially pop music.
3. A: We _____ a class movie in English.   B: Sounds good! You can be the director.
4. A: I don't like studying math.   B: Me _____.
5. A: I don't like watching foreign movies.   B: _____ do I. I don't like reading subtitles.

F **Use the Language**

How do you study?

1. How do you study? For example, do you like to work in groups or by yourself? Do you study in the mornings or evenings? Write three ways you like to study and three ways you don't like to study.

Like	Don't like
1.	1.
2.	2.
3.	3.

2. Tell a partner about how you study. Explain what you like and don't like while studying. Does your partner agree or disagree with you? Ask others. Did you find anybody who agrees with all the same things? Tell the class about the results.

Lesson 5 — Let's chat.

A Authentic Text: A chatroom

Read the messages on a social media site. Then answer the questions.

Andres, James, Samantha, Ivy
1:00 PM

Andres

Hi. I'm Andres. I want to study abroad. Is it a good idea? Has anybody done it? Tell me about your studies and any problems you had while abroad.

Hi, Andres. I lived in Toronto, Canada for one year. It was freezing there during winter, but summer was not too bad. I was in school during the weekdays, but relaxed on the weekends. There are many things to do there. If you like cycling, you'll love it. There were some good **cycling trails** around the city. You can rent bikes for a cheap price. You can also visit Niagara Falls and see the waterfall up close on a **cruise** or by helicopter. Yeah, so if you like nature and adventure, this is the place to go!

James

I did a semester of English at an **average-sized** college in Sydney. To be honest, it can be a real **drag** studying English all day. I needed a break from school. I went to lots of parties. I didn't study hard enough, but I met a lot of fun people. Oh, and if you like beaches or surfing on **gigantic** waves, you'll really like it in Sydney. The ocean there is **magnificent**!

Samantha

I studied in a small-town college near LA. It wasn't too busy, so I was able to concentrate on my studies. But it wasn't exciting enough for me, and I didn't meet many **locals**. I stayed with two other students. I was lonely because neither of them wanted to chat. I also became really **homesick**. Also, it can be expensive studying abroad. My advice is to do some research before going!

Ivy

Message   OK

1. Who didn't enjoy living abroad?   _____
2. Who didn't study much but made lots of friends?   _____
3. Who toured the city on the weekends?   _____

B Vocabulary

Write the bold words and phrases from part A next to the correct definitions.

1. _____ huge; very large
2. _____ very beautiful; amazing
3. _____ the people who live or who have lived in a place for a long time
4. _____ a long path for traveling on bicycles
5. _____ something dull and boring
6. _____ not too small or large
7. _____ a feeling of sadness caused by missing one's family and friends
8. _____ a tour by ship

C In Your World

How would you describe your school or college to a student from another country? Write some sentences about it on a separate sheet of paper. Share your description with a partner. Are your descriptions positive, negative, or both?

D Grammar

either, neither, and *both*; *too* and *enough* with adjectives

either + singular noun	*neither* + singular noun	*both* + plural noun
You can talk about two things using *both* (two positives), *neither* (two negatives), or *either* (choose one or the other one).		
Either place is good. (=Both are good.)	**Neither** student wanted to chat. (=Both didn't want to chat.)	I enjoyed **both** courses.

too + adjective	*not* + adjective + *enough*
Too and *enough* are adverbs, so they can describe adjectives or other adverbs. *Too* usually means "more than you want or need." *Enough* means "as much as you need."	
It was **too** quiet and **too** far from the shops. The city was **too** crowded for me.	It wasn't exciting **enough** for me. I didn't study hard **enough**.

Brief note
Look back to Lesson 2. The usage of *both A and B* and *both + plural noun* is the same.

Brief note
Too comes before the adjective or adverb, and *enough* comes after the adjective or adverb.

E Grammar Practice

Fill in the blanks with the correct words from the box.

either	neither	both	enough	too

1. I can find everything I want in the market and the shopping mall. I like _____ places.

2. The café and restaurant are old. _____ place has Wi-Fi, so I can't use the Internet there.

3. It's _____ hot in the movie theater. I never go there now.

4. The parks aren't safe _____ for me. I don't want to stay there after it gets dark.

5. The trains and buses are cheap. _____ one is good for students to use to get to school.

F Use the Language

Which city will be best?

1. Work in a group. Look at the cities described in Part A.

2. As a group, decide which city is the best place to study. You should do a little research about the city you have chosen. Then list 3 to 4 factors/reasons for your choice.

Which city?	Factors/Reasons
	•
	•
	•
	•

Tell the class about your choice and answer any questions they might have.

3. Which group presented the best ideas? Did you agree with the decisions made by each group?

A USA or Canada?

Listen to James talk to his friends about studying abroad. Fill in the blanks with the words you hear. 🎧 Track 42

Conversation 1: USA?

James: Hi, Anne. Thanks for calling me back. I just wanted to ask you about your time in LA.

Anne: Sure. Are you thinking about going there to study, too?

James: Yeah. Maybe. But I have a few questions before I decide. How _____ is it to study there?

Anne: Well, the school I went to was _____. It only cost about $1,000 per semester.

James: Oh. That's not too bad. Is it difficult to get into that school?

Anne: The _____ requirements are pretty low. You just need enough money and a good TOEFL score.

James: What's it like living there?

Anne: Um… the weather is hot most of the year, and it can become very humid in the summer. The traffic is bad, too.

James: Well, I'm not a fan of humid weather or waiting in traffic. Hmm… maybe I should just go to Canada.

Conversation 2: Canada?

James: Hi, Diane. This is James. So, when are you going back to study in Canada?

Diane: Oh, hi, James. I'm going back after summer vacation.

James: I see. I'm thinking about going to Toronto to study, too.

Diane: Really? Toronto's a really _____ city. I fell in love with it right away. It's a modern city with a lot of friendly _____.

James: Were you ever _____? I think I would miss my friends and family too much.

Diane: At first, I was. But after making new friends, I was fine.

James: That's great. What about the _____ and the food?

Diane: The nightlife is wonderful and there are plenty of awesome restaurants.

James: Speaking of food… Do you want to grab something to eat later?

Diane: Sure. I'm extremely hungry!

B Role-play

Read the conversations in groups of three. Then role-play the conversations again with different countries and cities. Use the Internet to learn more about the countries and cities you've chosen. What locations did your partners choose? Which one sounds most appealing to you? Share your best role-play with the class.

C Reminder

Some Module 4 Goals in Unit 8

Put a check mark (✓) next to the things you can do.

_____ Understand short, simple texts on familiar subjects

_____ Understand simple texts, emails, and letters

_____ Ask for and give opinions, agree, and disagree

Listen for Information

Listen to the description of a language school. Complete the information. `Track 43`

1. The school is in a _____ city.

2. It is less _____ _____ other big cities.

3. There are a lot of _____ _____ to do on the weekend.

4. You _____ _____ to the beach or visit _____ places.

5. The temperature is almost always _____.

6. We have dorms for _____ students.

7. There are a lot of group activities, such as _____ _____, _____, and city tours.

8. We have 260 students total, with _____ in each class.

9. Our campus is in the city center near _____ and _____.

10. It is _____ and _____ with Wi-Fi and facilities such as a _____, café, and study garden.

Discuss and Create

Your group has been asked to open a new language school (or university) in your city. Discuss where your school is and what facilities it has. Compare it to other schools in your city for international students. When you have agreed on your ideas, create a flyer, brochure, or PowerPoint presentation that describes your school.

Your school:	Other schools:
•	•
•	•
•	•
•	•
•	

Present

After you have created your presentation, work with another group. Show your presentation to the other group. Have them ask your group questions about your school and make suggestions. Make any necessary changes to your presentation. Then each group should present information about their school to the class.

A Vocabulary

Fill in the blanks with the correct words from the box.

main	nerves	homesick	greenest	backpacking	entry	especially
mood	beach	humid	dying to	high-tech	almost	affordable

1. I'm really _____ _____ eat something—I'm starving.

2. She has one coworker who really gets on her _____.

3. The school I went to was very _____. It only cost about $1000 dollars per semester.

4. You're in a really good _____ today. Is it because of this beautiful weather?

5. I fell in love with this city right away. I _____ love the great restaurants.

6. I've been _____ through Australia. The people were friendly and kind.

7. I often feel _____ when I am away. I miss my friends and family so much.

8. She doesn't feel well, so she'll have to skip our trip to the _____ today.

9. The weather is hot most of the year, and it can become very _____ in the summer.

10. The _____ requirements for the school are low.

11. Your major is your _____ course of study.

12. This city is one of the _____ cities in the world. There are many trees and parks.

13. There are a lot of _____ companies located in and around San Francisco, such as Facebook, Microsoft, and Apple.

14. I've memorized _____ all the vocabulary. Quiz me to see what I know.

B Grammar

Fill in the blanks with the correct words from the box.

as	both	during	ever	few	fewer	for	long	
less	most	neither	none	since	too	whether		

1. How _____ have you studied English?

2. Have you _____ been to Mexico?

3. She has lived here _____ ten years.

4. I haven't seen her _____ we went to the party.

5. _____ of those three movies are good. They're all boring!

6. A _____ of the students came—I think about three or four.

7. I went traveling _____ the holidays.

8. I'm not sure _____ to stay or transfer next semester.

9. New York is the _____ international city in the world!

10. The shopping center is _____ crowded in the morning. I always come then.

11. _____ Miami and Seattle are great cities to study. They're awesome!

12. _____ student wanted to talk. They were very tired.

13. They're the same price. This shirt is _____ expensive as that shirt.

14. There are _____ students in the class today than yesterday.

15. It's _____ hot to study today.

C Conversation

Put the conversation in the correct order. Then listen and check. 🔘 Track 44

<u> 1 </u> Hi, Alex. How was your time abroad? Has your English improved since the last time I saw you?

_____ Canada? I guess if you like freezing temperatures and snow. I prefer hot and humid weather.

_____ Well, Canada is a possibility. I've always wanted to go there. I've heard the large cities are modern and high-tech, but the smaller cities are greener and quieter.

_____ Of course! I've been overseas for four semesters, so my pronunciation and vocabulary have improved a lot.

_____ You're so lucky. I was thinking about studying abroad too. I haven't made up my mind yet.

_____ Where do you want to go?

_____ I see. Well, if it includes everything, I guess it's not too bad.

_____ Um…it depends on where you go to study. But the average cost is about $20,000.

_____ Well, me too. But I think I can adjust to the cold. And it'd be nice to live in a different place for a while. Anyway, how much does it cost to study for a year?

_____ Wow. That's so expensive.

_____ You should research different schools and cities to help you figure it out. That's what I did.

_____ Yeah, but that includes the cost for staying in the dorm and meals. It can be cheaper if you decide to stay with a homestay family.

<u>13</u> Maybe I'll do that tonight. Anyway, it was nice to catch up with you. Thanks for helping out.

D Where will we study abroad?

Role-play a conversation with a friend. Imagine you are taking a semester or year off from studying. Discuss the pros and cons of going home, traveling for fun or to volunteer, and getting a job. Choose the best option for you. Tell other students about your choice and your reasons for doing it.

	Pros	Cons
Going home		
Traveling for fun		
Traveling to volunteer		
Getting a job		

E Anna's Email

This is Anna. She finally decided to study abroad at a language school. She has been studying abroad for about a month. She has decided to write to one of her friends back home. Imagine that you are Anna. On a separate piece of paper, write an email to her friend. Make sure to write about all of the photos in your email.

Lesson 1 Present continuous for future plans

We use this tense to talk about what we are going to do in the future.

Use subject + *be* + verb-*ing* + time phrase.

He's traveling to Lima this summer.
I'm working tomorrow.

subject	be	verb + -ing (+ object)	future time phrase*
I	am	taking a class	in May.
He / She / It	is	going to L.A.	next week.
You / We / They	are	visiting Rob	after school.

Note In real life, people do not always use the time phrases. Context after makes the time clear.

Lesson 2 Simple present vs. present continuous

Simple present is for routines or scheduled actions. Present continuous describes what's happening now or future plans.

Simple present = subject + present verb.

Present continuous = subject + be + verb + -ing

I often go jogging.   They're talking on the phone now.

	simple present	present continuous
present meaning	generally true; routine or habitual	happening at the time of speaking
examples	He usually **volunteers**. She **studies** at home at night.	He**'s volunteering** right now. She**'s studying** at home at the moment.
time expressions	every day, week, month, morning, afternoon in the morning, afternoon, evening usually, often, never	right now at the moment
future meaning	scheduled actions	plans
examples	My train **arrives** at 10:05 a.m. today. My job **begins** on June 25th.	I**'m meeting** Dave at the career center today. We**'re going** to a party on Saturday night.

Lesson 3 Gerunds and infinitives; conjunction *because*

Gerunds and infinitives come after certain verbs. We use *because* to join ideas and *still* to describe continuation.

Use subject + verb + gerund/infinitive.

I still don't like to eat pizza because it doesn't taste good.

verbs followed by gerunds (verb + -ing)	verbs followed by infinitives (to + verb)	verbs followed by both
enjoy finish quit dislike practice	learn need want promise decide	hate like love can't stand
I **dislike** watch**ing** sports. He **quit** work**ing** at the shop.	She **promised to go** with me. We **need to buy** new books.	I **love** swimm**ing**. I **love to be** outdoors.

using *because* to give a reason	
because clause, clause (comma needed)	**Because** Grandpa loves to exercise, he's still healthy and strong.
clause + *because* clause (no comma needed)	Grandpa's still healthy and strong **because** he loves to exercise.

Lesson 4 Future with *will*; want / *would like* + object + infinitive

Will is used to express future time. It is used to express possibilities, offers, and decisions. When speaking, use the contracted form of *will*.

Use *will* + base verb.

I will go to the park tomorrow.   I'll help you.

using *will* to express future time: *will* + base verb	
possibilities	It's cloudy. I think it **will rain** this afternoon.
offers	The phone is ringing. I**'ll answer** it.
decisions made when speaking	That looks like a nice place to visit. Maybe we**'ll go** there next month.

We use *want* and *would like* to describe what we desire.

Use *want* + N / to verb / object to be less formal and *would like* + N / to verb / object to be more formal.

I'd like to travel.   He wants you to close the door.

expressing preferences with *want / would like*	
with a noun phrase	*Less formal:* I **want** a hamburger. *More formal:* I **would like** a hamburger (please).
with an infinitive	*Less formal:* I **want** to be a chef. *More formal:* I **would like** to be a chef.
with an object + to verb	*Less formal:* Terry **wants** me to quit. *More formal:* Terry **would like** me to quit.

Lesson 5 Questions with *why* and answers; conjunction *so*

Questions with *why* are used to ask for reasons. You can answer *Why*-questions by using *because* or an infinitive.

We use *so* to give reasons or consequences. Use *so* + reason/consequence.

I'm online so I can find a program.

asking for reasons with *why*	
question	answer
Why are you going to college?	**Because** I want to get a job. I'm going to college **because** I want to get a good job.
	To get a good job. / I'm going to college **to get** a good job.

using *so*	
to give a reason	I'm going to college **so (that)** I can get a good job. Hugo gets up early in the morning **so (that)** he is not late for work.
to state a result	Kim was really late for work, **so** her boss got angry. I'm tired of studying, **so** I'm taking a short break.

Unit 2
Researching Your Options

Lesson 1 *have to*

We use *have to* when we talk about something we need to do.

Use subject + *have/has/had* + *to* + verb.

He has to change his cover letter.   I had to discuss my skills.

subject + (present tense) *have to* + verb (base) and extra information		
I / You / We / They	have to don't have to	hunt for a new job.
He / She / It	has to doesn't have to	write a résumé.
(past tense) *had to*	had to didn't have to	ask the boss for a
(All subjects)		reference.

Lesson 2 *have to* and *must*

We use *have to* and *must* when we talk about necessary things. We use *must not* for rules and *don't have to* for choices.

Use subject + *have to* / *must* or *don't have to* / *must not* + verb.

Applicants don't have to have a degree.
He must be early.

	have to + verb	*must* + verb	meaning
+	I **have to** send my transcripts. (This is necessary.)	I **must** send my transcripts. (This is necessary.)	same
-	You **don't have to** have experience to apply for this job. (You have a choice.)	Candidates **must not** forget a cover letter (They do not have a choice. It is a rule.)	opposite

Lesson 3 *may* and *might*

We use *may (not)* / *might (not)* to talk about future possibility.

Use subject + *may (not)* / *might (not)* + base verb.

I might change my accommodations.
He may not graduate.

possibility or future prediction	*may* or *might* + base verb
may **might**	They **may** live in a dormitory. (50%) She **might** quit school this semester. (50%)
may not **might not**	I **may not** take that biology course. (50%) You **might not** like this professor. (50%)

Lesson 4 *maybe, perhaps,* and *probably*

Use *possibly, perhaps,* and *probably* for future predictions.

Use subject + *possibly/probably* + verb.

We probably will have an exam in April.

Use *perhaps* + subject + verb.

Perhaps he'll win.

% of probability	use *may* or *might* after subject	use *possibly* after subject	use *perhaps* before subject
50% chance	I **might** check out the library. He **may not** get employment.	I'll **possibly** check out the library. He **possibly won't** get employment.	**Perhaps** I'll check out the library. **Perhaps** he won't get employment.
more than 50% chance	use *probably* after subject		
	His reputation will **probably** get better. They **probably** won't be able to pay the tuition.		

Lesson 5 Intensifiers

We use intensifiers to describe the strength of an adjective or verb.

Use subject + verb + intensifier + adjective (+ noun) or verb.

This seascape is really fantastic!   I'm definitely leaving soon.

intensifier		after a linking verb	before a noun
mild	*quite* *fairly* *rather*	The campus is **quite** beautiful. Daniel's **fairly** fun.	The campus is **quite** a beautiful place. Daniel's a **fairly** fun guy.
strong	*such* *very* *really* *so*	This homestay isn't very **nice**. The entertainment here is so **exciting**!	It isn't a **very** nice homestay. I've got **such** a jealous roommate.
very strong	*extremely* *definitely* *completely* *totally*	Sarah's party was **extremely** loud. Your university is **definitely** better.	Sarah had an **extremely** loud party. Your university is **definitely** a better school.
Sometimes, verbs can follow *really, definitely, completely, totally*.		She **really** loves going overseas. They **totally** succeeded. John's **definitely** moving to a multicultural neighborhood.	

119

Unit 3

Basics of the Process

Lesson 1 Phrasal verbs

Phrasal verbs have a verb and then another element, such as an adverb (*break down*) or preposition (*talk about*). They are usually used informally. There are two types: inseparable and separable.

Inseparable phrasal verbs cannot have an object between the verb and other element. Separable phrasal verbs can have an object between the verb and other element.

I need to go over my class notes before the exam.

I need to look them up in my notebook.

	examples	sentences
inseparable	*get on, go over*	I don't want to **get on** that bus; it's too crowded! You should **go over** new vocabulary every night.
separable	*fill out, look up*	Please **fill out** a job application. You can **fill it out** online. A lot people use the Internet to **look up** things they don't know. **Looking them up** in books is not popular anymore.

Note Phrasal verbs can be used in any verb tense, just like regular verbs.

Note The phrasal verb *get on* works with some types of transportation: plane, bus, bicycle, train, metro, and boat. *Get in* is used with taxis and cars.

Lesson 2 *prefer* + noun, gerund, or infinitive

The verb *prefer* can be followed by a noun, a gerund, or an infinitive. There is no difference in meaning.

prefer + (not) *noun / gerund / infinitive*… come after the subject.

I prefer coffee in the morning.

I prefer drinking coffee in the morning.

I prefer to drink coffee in the morning.

prefer + noun	We **prefer online applications**. I **prefer** group work.
prefer + gerund	We **prefer receiving** online applications. I **prefer** (not) working in a group.
prefer + infinitive	We **prefer to receive** online applications. I **prefer (not) to work** in a group.

Lesson 3 Advice with *should*, imperatives, and (*would*) *suggest/recommend* + gerund

There are many ways to give advice in English, including using *should*, imperative verbs, and *suggest* + gerund.

Subject + *should* + (*not*) + verb…

Imperative

Subject + (*would*) + *suggest* + (*not*) + gerund…

You shouldn't be late for your interview.
I would suggest wearing a suit.
Don't forget to write a thank you letter.

should + verb	You **should wait** for us to call you next week. You **shouldn't wear** sandals to the office.
imperative	**Don't be** late for the meeting. **Don't use** social media during work hours.
(*would*) + *suggest* + (*not*) + gerund	I **would suggest making** some changes to your resume. I **suggest** not taking the bus after 10 p.m.

Note *Should* is polite and can be used between coworkers and friends. Imperatives are less polite and are used when giving instructions. *Suggest* is quite formal and is used in writing and polite conversations.

Lesson 4 *I know* + clause; conjunction *before*

Use *I know* (*that*) + clause to talk about things you know. The conjunction *before* is like glue between two parts of a sentence to show that one thing happens at an earlier time than another.

Start the sentence with: I know (*that*) + clause.

I know (*that*) + clause
I know (that) the job description was posted yesterday. **I didn't know** they had hired a new department head.

The conjunction *before* can come before or after another clause. The clause with *before* talks about what happens later. The other clause tells what happens earlier.

Either start the sentence with Before + clause,… or end it with … before + clause.

Before we meet, let me read your resume.

Let me read your resume before we meet.

Before + clause
Before you go, give me your business card. Remember to submit your application **before** January 31st.

Lesson 5 Infinitives in common phrases

Infinitives are used with several common phrases.

After the subject, add *need to / be able to / know how to / in order to* + infinitive.

need to + infinitive	I need to set up a meeting with all the directors this week. You don't need to send me an email.
be able to + infinitive	Will you be able to finish this work today? I'm not able to meet with you today.
know how to + infinitive	I know how to speak French. I don't know how to fix the printer.
in order to + infinitive	I need to use the computer in order to finish this project.

Lesson 1 — Object pronouns and reflexive pronouns

Object pronouns can be used instead of a person's name or thing as the object of the verb or preposition. Use reflexive pronouns when the subject and object are the same.

Subject + verb + (preposition) object/reflexive pronoun.

object pronouns	singular	plural
	I = **me** you = **you** he = **him** she = **her** it = **it**	we = **us** they = **them**
	My mother is very proud of **me**. Please call **us** for an interview next week.	

reflexive pronouns	singular	plural
	I = **myself** you = **yourself** he = **himself** she = **herself** it = **itself**	we = **ourselves** they = **themselves**
	The lights turn off by **themselves**. She lives by **herself** in a small apartment.	

Lesson 2 — Simple past of *be*; *be like*

Was and *were* are the past forms of the verb *be*. It is common to add *there* to give facts about the past.

There + was/were (no) + subject...

Subject + was/were (not)...

There were many people absent at the office today.

statements	There **was**... There **were**...	I / He / She / It **was**... You / We / They **were**...
	There **was** a cafe here before. We **were** at the zoo yesterday.	
questions	There **was**...? There **were**...?	**Was** I / he / she / it...? **Were** you / we / they...?
	There **was** cake at the party? **Were** you nervous before the interview?	
negatives	There **wasn't**... There **weren't**...	I / He / She / It **wasn't**... You / We / They **weren't**...
	There **weren't** any open positions. She **wasn't** the best applicant for the job.	

You can use *be like* to ask someone to describe something. Start with *What*, then *be* verb + subject + *like*?

questions with *be like*		
future tense	**present tense**	**past tense**
What **will** your schedule **be** like?	What **is** your office **like**?	What **was** college **like**?

Lesson 3 — Simple past: regular verbs

Regular verbs are verbs that take -(e)d at the end when using the simple past.

Subject + verb + -(e)d...

regular verbs	verb + -(e)d	decided, managed, wondered
regular verbs that end in -y	change -y to -i and add -ed	copied, cried, studied
regular verbs with a single stressed vowel before a single final consonant	double the final consonant and add -ed	stopped, preferred, planned

Note There are many verbs that end in -y that do not take -ied in the simple past. This is because they have a vowel before ending in -y. Examples: play = played; employ = employed; stay = stayed

Lesson 4 — Simple past: irregular verbs

Irregular verbs do not take -(e)d in the simple past. They must be memorized.

Subject + simple past irregular verb...

irregular verbs	read = read think = thought know = knew	I **began** my career in 2001. She **left** early for her doctor's appointment. I **took** his business card.

Lesson 5 — *when* clauses in future statements

When can be used to introduce a clause that describes something that will happen at a specific time in the future. The *when* clause uses the simple present and must have a subject and verb. It must be used with another clause.

When + clause (subject + simple present verb), clause (subject + future tense verb).

Clause (subject + future tense verb) + *when* + clause (subject + simple present verb).

When I go to college, I will study graphic design.
I will study graphic design when I go to college.

When + clause...	**When** I get a job, I will buy a new car. **When** he doesn't hear from you, he will be worried. **When** I come, will you still be there?
...when + clause.	I will call you **when** I am free. Lucy will be happy to see you **when** you are here. Will you buy some oranges **when** you go shopping?

Unit 5

Changing Your Major

Lesson 1 Zero conditional

A zero conditional sentence is an *if* sentence that expresses something generally true. It has an *if* clause (expressing a condition) and result clause. Both clauses are in the simple present tense.

If I don't eat, I get tired.

zero conditional	
if clause	result clause
If students **don't study,**	they **fail** class.
If you **have** a college degree,	you **have** a better chance at finding a job.
If you **save** money,	you **can buy** a car.

Lesson 2 Infinitives of purpose; *in order to*

We use *to*-infinitives to express purpose. *In order (not) to* is also used to express purpose.

He's going to college to get a master's degree.

The school president gave a speech in order to set new rules.

infinitives of purpose	
usage	examples
An infinitive (*to* + verb) often states the purpose of an action.	**To improve your dance technique,** you should practice every day.
In order to is another common way to express purpose. It sounds a bit more formal.	She went to a book fair **in order to buy a poetry book.**
In order not to is the correct way to express a negative purpose.	**In order not to be late for class,** I ran to school.

Lesson 3 *be good/bad at; help* + object + *(to)* verb

We use *be good/bad at* to express something we do/don't do well.

He is good at speaking English.
She is bad at playing the flute.

be good/bad at + noun	*be good/bad at* + gerund
She **is good at interior design.** He**'s bad at management.** I**'m** not very **good at math.**	She **is good at drawing.** He**'s bad at solving** problems. I**'m** not very **good at dancing.**

The verb *help* can be followed by an object + *(to)* verb.

My professor helped me to finish my science project.

help + object + *(to)* verb
My mother **helped me to study.** Nobody **helped Sam pay** for college. Please **us her find** the cafeteria.

Lesson 4 *would rather*

We use *would rather* to compare or choose things.

I would rather eat pizza than eat a hamburger
Would you rather major in finance or programming?
She would rather not study off campus.

would rather + verb		
comparing two options	*would rather* + verb... + *than*...	I **would rather** play the flute **than** sing. She**'d rather** take a photography class **than** learn design.
questions	*Would* S *rather* + verb... + *or*...?	**Would** you **rather see** a movie **or** go bowling?
using context	We can use *would rather* with only one option when we know the other option.	A: Do you want to study in the library? B: No, I**'d rather study** at home.
would rather not	S *would rather not* + verb. (There are no options; the subject simply doesn't want to.)	We **would rather not** stay at the party longer than two hours. (= We don't want to...)

Lesson 5 *other* and *another; else*

We use *other/another* with nouns and *else* in question form.

Our college has more graduates than other colleges.
I move to another university.
What else can I bring to the party?

other and *another*	*else*
Other is often used with plural nouns. *Another* is only used with singular nouns. (Note that *another* contains the article *an*. This should remind you that it is used for singular nouns.)	*Else* is used after the question words *how, what, where, who,* and *why* to mean "more," "other," or "different."
Our university offers lower tuition than **other** universities. I want to change to **another** major.	A: Mike is going to the school seminar. B: Good. Who **else** is going? I don't like this medicine. What **else** I can take?

Unit 6
Transferring

Lesson 1 Adverbs of place

We use adverbs of place to give the location or direction of an action. They are used after the object or main verb.

I walked around.

adverbs of place
Like prepositions of place, adverbs of place tell us where something happens. They are different from prepositions of place because they do not have to be followed by a noun. They usually come after the object or the main verb.
We looked **around**, but we couldn't find our car. I ran **outside**. There is another supermarket **there**. We will go **inside**.

Lesson 2 *had better* (**not**) and *let's*

We use *had better* to make suggestions to avoid negative results.

My son forgot his lunch. I had better bring him some food.

We use *let's* to make suggestions for plans.

Let's make a date for this weekend.

had better (**not**) + verb for suggestions and warnings	
Use *had better* to talk about things that someone should do. This is a strong way of making a suggestion. It has the meaning that there might be a negative result if the person does not do the action.	
+	You're sick. You **had better go** to bed. He needs money. He**'d better get** a job.
-	She's sleeping. You**'d better not call** her.
let's + verb for suggestions and proposals	
Use *let's* to make suggestions or proposals to someone, especially about something you can do together. It is a contraction of "Let us".	
Let's go downtown for dinner. **Let's have** a look at some brochures.	

Lesson 3 First conditional; *have* + object + *to* verb

We use the first conditional to talk about events that may happen in the future.

If he gets into Yale, he'll be excited.

She will pay tuition if she gets the loan tomorrow.

first conditional	
A first conditional is an *if* sentence that expresses something that will be true in the future. It has an *if* clause in the simple present tense and result clause in the future tense.	
if clause (simple present) + result (*will* + verb)	**If** it **snows**, I will wear a hat. **If** you sleep, you**'ll be** rested.
result (*will* + verb) + *if* clause (simple present)	They **will** go and see a movie **if** it **is not** too late.
have + object + *to* verb	
Use *have* + object + *to* verb to talk about things that people own or possess. These can be physical objects or ideas.	
I **have a chance to audition** for the musical.	

Lesson 4 *think* + (**that**) clause

We use *think* to express uncertain opinions and facts.

I think that he should eat more vegetables.

subject + *think* + (**that**) clause
Use this structure to give opinions or facts that you are unsure about.
I **think (that) I should exercise every day**. My mother **thinks (that) I am a genius**. What do **you think (that) I should buy**? Kelly thinks **(that) you should** buy a new backpack.

Lesson 5 *keep/continue* + gerund; *why not* and *why don't*

We use *keep/continue* + gerund for actions that continue to reach a goal.

If he wants to pass chemistry, he has to continue studying with a tutor.

keep/continue + gerund	
Use this structure to talk about an action that you continue to do, often to reach a specific goal.	
If you want to get better at guitar, you have to **keep practicing**.	If you want to lose weight, you have to **continue exercising** and eating less.
Keep trying if you want to get into a good university.	**Continue singing** if you want to be a professional.

Why not...? and *Why don't...?* are used to make suggestions.

Why don't we drive to the beach?

why don't + *why not*
Use these phrases (*why don't* + subject + verb...?; *why not* + verb...?) to make suggestions.
Why don't you take a semester off? **Why doesn't he make** a budget?
Why not leave the house earlier? **Why not apply** for the job?

Lesson 1 Present perfect; *still, never,* and *yet*

The present perfect is often used to talk about experiences: things that happened (or didn't happen) at an unspecific time in the past. To form the present perfect, use *have/has* + past participle. For regular verbs, the past participle is the same as the simple past form.

I've never read his blog.   He still hasn't taken time off.

present perfect: *has/have* + past participle		
statements	**negative statements**	**questions and short answers**
I **have traveled** / I**'ve traveled** abroad.	He **has not / hasn't volunteered** at the library.	**Have** you **traveled** abroad? Yes, I **have**. / No, I **haven't**.
adverbs used with the present perfect		
still	**never**	**yet**
I **still** haven't cooked dinner.	Ian has **never** studied chemistry.	I haven't cooked dinner **yet**.

Lesson 2 Simple past vs. present perfect; *few* vs. *a few; none of* + ...

We use simple past for actions at specific times in the past. We use present perfect for past actions at unspecified times.

past simple	present perfect
Simple past describes actions at *specific* times in the past.	Present perfect describes past actions with no specific time.
I **studied** last night.	I**'ve studied** a lot.

Few and *none* describe quantities and go before an object.

I saw a few movies last month.

None of the students have talked to me.

few vs. *a few; none of* + ...	
Few means "not many," and *a few* means "some." *None of* means "not one" or "not any."	
few + plural noun	**none** + pronoun / (det.) + noun
few students **a few** classes	**none** of them **none** of the options

Lesson 3 Time expressions with the present perfect; empty *it*

To talk about a period of time, use *for, in,* or *since* with the present perfect. Use empty *it* when there's no clear subject.

It has rained for three days.

She hasn't worked since 2015.

present perfect + *for* + period of time	present perfect + *in* + period of time
I've played soccer **for a long time**.	I haven't taken a break **in months**.
since + event/time	*since* + S + V
You can use since to say how long ago something began.	
They've lived in Hong Kong **since 2015**.	I haven't talked to him **since we had dinner last week**.
empty *it*	
You can use empty *it* as a subject in sentences about the weather, dates, distances, etc.	
It will snow tomorrow. **It**'s been nice seeing you!	**It**'s Monday, May 19. How far is **it** to the library?

Note *For* and *in* have the same meaning here, but we use *in* only in negative sentences. In positive sentences, both are okay.

Lesson 4 *ever, never,* and *always; while* and *during*

We use *ever, never,* and *always* to give more details. We use *during* and *while* to describe actions happening at the same time.

Have you ever been to Brazil?

I slept during the movie.

present perfect with *ever/never/always*	
Have you **ever** gone backpacking? I've **never** littered. She has **always** wanted to help out.	
during + noun	*while* + clause
Both *during* + noun and *while* + clause say that something is happening at the same time as something else.	
Where did you go **during** your vacation?	He'll help me out **while** I'm doing my research.

Lesson 5 *How long* questions with the present perfect; *so far*

We use *how long* questions to find out the duration of an activity. We answer with *since/for* and a time expression. *So far* is used to say "up until now, and maybe after that."

How long have you been a waiter?

Since May. I like it so far.

How long + present perfect questions
Use *How long* + present perfect to ask about the period of time something has lasted, from the beginning until now. The answer often uses *since* or *for*.
A: **How long** has he taught?   B: **Since** 2003. / For two years.
so far
So far means "up until now and maybe after that."
I've enjoyed the job **so far**.   **So far**, she's happy.

Unit 8
Studying Abroad

Lesson 1 *whether* and *if*

To discuss two options, we use *whether* or *if*.
She's not sure if she should stay put or go out tonight.

whether (option 1 *or* option 2)	if (option 1 *or* option 2)
We can use *whether/if... or...* to talk about two options or possibilities.	
Do you know **whether** this school is suitable **or** not? I don't know **whether** the nightlife is better here **or** in LA.	I'm not sure **if** he's a fan of football **or** baseball. Have you decided **if** you'll study biology **or** physics?

Note When you have two possibilities, it is better to use *whether* because *if* can change the meaning of the sentence.

Lesson 2 Comparative and superlative adjectives: *more/most, less/least; both* A *and* B

Comparatives compare two things. Superlatives describe the greatest or lowest degree. We use *both* to include two things.
This school's more high tech than yours.
This city is the most affordable in the area.
I like both Sue and Li.

comparative adjectives (A *is less/more* + adjective *than* B)	superlative adjectives (A *is the least/most* + adjective)
Comparatives compare two things. Less is the opposite of more.	Superlatives describe the greatest or lowest degree. Least is the opposite of most.
The gallery is **less interesting than** the national museum. California's beaches are **more beautiful than** Florida's.	Did you know they have **the least healthy** diet? It has the **most expensive** housing in the state.

both A *and* B
When you use *both* A *and* B, remember that A and B must be the same type or part of speech (noun, verb, infinitive, etc.).
You will enjoy **both** the sports **and** the theater in this city. I need to **both** study **and** explore while I live abroad.

Lesson 3 Comparing using *less, fewer,* and (*not*) *as... as...*

We use (*not*) *as... as...*, *less,* and *fewer* to compare things.
This food isn't as tasty as mine. I have fewer exams this year.

less + adjective / uncountable noun	fewer + countable noun
Less is used to compare adjectives and uncountable nouns. *Fewer* is used to compare countable nouns. Both words mean the opposite of *more*.	
A dorm feels **less** comfortable than a house. Atlanta has **less** traffic than New York.	Calgary has **fewer** homestays than Toronto. **Fewer** cultural events happen there.

as + adjective + as
You can use *as... as...* to say two things are the same or *not as... as...* to describe their differences.
His campus is **as** modern **as** her campus. My new city is **not as** affordable **as** my old city. This school has **as many** entry requirements **as** that one.

Note When you want to say one thing is less than another, you can either use *less than* or *not as...as*. Also, *Not as many...as* has the same meaning as *fewer...than*.

Lesson 4 *can/could* for possibility; phrases for agreement

We use *can* and *could* to talk about things that are possible.
We can walk together.   I could meet you at the café.
We respond to statements with phrases of agreement.
A: I like old movies.   B: Me too!

can/can't + base verb	could + base verb
We use *can* and *could* to talk about possible things.	
We **can** grab dinner downtown before the party.	You **could** watch the movie with subtitles.
phrases for agreement	
You can use *so, too,* and *neither* to say that you agree with someone.	
agreeing with a positive sentence	agreeing with a negative sentence
So do I. / Yeah, me too.	Neither do I. / Me neither!
A: I want to invite Sue over. B: Yeah, so do I.	A: I can't dance at all. B: Me neither.

Lesson 5 *either, neither,* and *both*; using *too* and *enough* with adjectives

We use *either, neither,* and *both* to talk about two things. We use *too* and *enough* with adjectives to describe amounts.
You can apply to either college.
Both colleges are excellent.

either + singular noun	neither + singular noun	both + plural noun
You can talk about two things using *both* (two positives), *neither* (two negatives), or *either* (choose one or the other one).		
Either restaurant is fine.	**Neither** girl was friendly.	I took **both** classes.
too + adjective		not + adjective + enough
Too adjective means "more than you want or need." *Enough* + adjective means "as much as you need."		
This town is **too** boring.		It wasn't warm **enough**.

Unit 1
What to Do

Lesson 1
experience
field
gap year
nanny
student loan
apply
run
volunteer
think (of/about)

Lesson 2
appointment
cover letter
employment
expert
government
job fair
job interview
résumé
local
get in touch with

Lesson 3
decision
IT (information technology)
outdoors
recreation leader
tough
worried
can't stand
look into

Lesson 4
actor
architect
architecture
carpenter
carpentry
chef
culinary arts
doctor
education
medicine
teacher
theater arts

Lesson 5
break
brochure
baking
ironing clothes
scrubbing
vacuuming

dog-sit
research
tired of

Unit 2
Researching Your Options

Lesson 1
ability
application
duties
job hunting
position
reference
tip
accept
hire
search
boring
challenging
fascinating
frightening
hard-working
interesting

Lesson 2
applicant
assistant
documents
grade
transcript
academic
excellent
successful
valuable
motivated
organized
self-directed
register
submit

Lesson 3
course
decision
location
MBA
prediction
quality
reputation
decide (on)
abroad

Lesson 4
academy
categories

facilities
faculty
province
rate

Lesson 5
destination
entertainment
homestay
overseas
residents
scenery
sea
saint (St.)
jealous
located
tiny
definitely

Unit 3
Basics of the Process

Lesson 1
administration
corporation (Corp.)
data
hours
qualification
contact
prefer
permanent
previous
temporary

Lesson 2
human resources
noon
preference
strength
appreciate
suit
administrative
look forward to

Lesson 3
first impression
outfit
arrive
confirm
forget
recommend
suggest
plenty
a bit
guess what

Lesson 4
professional development
helpful
outstanding
establish
hope
supply

Lesson 5
art director
brand
client
communications director
content developer
department head
job description
marketing associate
project
project manager
web designer
closely
familiar with
in charge of

Unit 4
Deeper into the Interview

Lesson 1
accomplishment
challenge
weakness
willing
face
memorize
prepare
relocate
respond
come up

Lesson 2
background
cons
deadline
overtime
pros
teamwork
trends
describe
easygoing
encouraging
entry-level
come up with

Lesson 3
benefit
certificate

correspondence
phase
society
manage
realize
useful

Lesson 4
attitude
confidence
salary
lie
seek
wonder
unfortunately
bring up

Lesson 5
candidate
department
starting date
long-term
someday
hear from
work on
wrap up

Unit 5
Changing Your Major

Lesson 1
factor
interest
opportunities
program
situation
avoid
offer
competitive

Lesson 2
advertising
politics
products
professions
relations
similarities
theory
assist
social
undergraduate

Lesson 3
detail
knowledge
passions

argue
motivate
persuade
spend
legal
else

Lesson 4
African-American history
finance
forestry
graphic design
hospitality management
interior design
programming
travel and tourism
by
catch up with

Lesson 5
therapy
psych
support
switch
trust
generous
practical
related
finally

Unit 6
Transferring

Lesson 1
access
convenience
credit
downtown
east
environment
healthcare
north
satisfaction
south
west
enroll
transfer
around
back
everywhere
inside
nearby
outside
get into

Lesson 2
environmental science
physical therapy
statistics
TESOL
warning
fail
intense
limited
have a look

Lesson 3
assistance
finance
continuing education
faculty
humanities
life sciences
discover
experience
inspire

Lesson 4
recruiter
surrounding community
browse
visit
wander
find out
make an inquiry
sit in on
a bunch of
How about / What about…?

Lesson 5
budget
culture
embassy
exchange program
insurance
visa
combine
take… off
…and stuff

Unit 7
Time Off

Lesson 1
blog
possibility
earn
waste
homeless
whole

figure out
pros and cons

Lesson 2
advisor
adjust (to)
uncertain
get on (one's) nerves
make up (one's) mind
stay put
more and more

Lesson 3
beach
mood
mention
busy
lazy
almost
especially
catch up (with)
dying (to)

Lesson 4
climbing
dolphin
national park
planting
sailing
sightseeing
litter
post

Lesson 5
advancement
customer service
IT skill
leadership
organization
tip
wage
provide

Unit 8
Studying Abroad

Lesson 1
nightlife
freezing
main
suitable
extremely
seriously
thoroughly
be a fan of
Toronto
San Diego

Lesson 2

festival
green
high-tech
historic
year-round
fall in love

Lesson 3

cultural event
entry requirement
survey
traffic
affordable
comfortable
modern

Lesson 4

pronunciation
subtitle
Wi-Fi
download
grab
quiz
skip
convenient
free of charge

Lesson 5

cruise
cycling trail
drag
homesick
locals
average-sized
gigantic
magnificent